EASY TO MAKE
CROSS STITCH
PICTURES

EASY TO MAKE

CROSS STITCH
PICTURES

Julia Jones and Barbara Deer

Brockhampton Press
LONDON

First published in Great Britain in 1993
by Anaya Publishers Ltd, Strode House,
44-50 Osnaburgh Street, London NW1 3ND

This edition published 1996 by Brockhampton Press,
a member of Hodder Headline PLC Group

Editor Eve Harlow
Design by Design 23
Photography Steve Tanner
Charts Line + Line
Anthony Duke
Illustrator Kate Simunek

British Library Cataloguing in Publication Data

Jones, Julia
Easy to make Cross Stitch Picures. – (Easy to make Series)
I. Title II. Deer, Barbara III. Series
746.44
ISBN 1-86019-139-8

Typeset by Servis Filmsetting Ltd, Manchester, UK
Colour reproduction by Scantrans Pte Ltd, Singapore
Printed and bound in EC

CONTENTS

Introduction

Cross stitch can be found all over the world in countries as far apart as Mexico and India, Greece and Thailand. The same simple techniques have been practised for thousands of years.

Cross stitching was probably the first effective method of lacing animal skins together to make body coverings and sleeping covers. Gradually, with the development of hand-woven fabrics, cross stitch evolved into a stitch which was decorative as well as functional.

No-one knows exactly where cross stitch originated. The Crusaders brought embroidered textiles back to the west after the Crusades and cross stitch would have been on the textiles. Embroidery craftsmen worked the trade routes across the middle east and Europe, taking the skills wherever they settled and this must have helped to familiarize westerners with eastern embroidery stitches.

However, if you spend a little time studying international embroidery designs you will be fascinated to see similar cross stitch motifs occurring in embroideries of countries as far apart as Mexico and Greece, Hungary and Thailand.

In sixteenth-century Europe, all forms of embroidery, including cross stitch, were exceedingly popular. Embroidery was worked for pleasure by ladies and noblewomen of the royal courts. Professional designers travelled the country, making patterns for use on bed-hangings, linens, clothing and accessories for adornment.

Skill with a needle was also considered to be of prime importance in the education of young girls and, together with music and painting, was a great asset for a prospective wife.

Origins of samplers

The samplers of this time, worked on linen cloth, were very charming in design although sometimes naive in concept. Early examples were known as 'random' or 'spot' samplers and designs were scattered over the fabric with no attempt at symmetry. Some of these strips of fabric, covered with motifs and blocks of stitches, are up to 24in (60cm) long.

By the 17th century, the random method of working samplers had disappeared, replaced by designs of alphabets and numbers, flowers and figures.

The sampler as we know it today came into being in the 18th century, with cross stitch as the predominant stitch. It continued in popularity until, by the 19th century, rows of numbers and alphabets began to be replaced by religious and uplifting texts.

Luckily, today's needleworkers are able to enjoy cross stitch – and making samplers – as a relaxing and highly enjoyable leisure occupation.

Quick to learn

Cross stitch is extremely easy to do and most people, men and women and children too, usually master it in about an hour. It is possible for someone who has never before worked an embroidery stitch to produce a piece of cross stitching that looks as good as that produced by an expert. Because it is so easy, and so relaxing to do, cross stitch is now becoming the most popular needlecraft in the western world. Most people begin with a small motif or a picture that they can complete in one evening. Later, they go on to work bigger pieces.

Something for everyone

We intended this book of cross stitch pictures to be something that everyone could enjoy, not just experienced needleworkers but also those thousands of people who would love to do embroidery, if only they knew how.

If you are one of these, then this is where you start doing one of the most fascinating needlecrafts in the world,

using a simple stitch that women (and men) have been working for thousands of years.

In this book, there is just about every kind of picture anyone could want. The Flowers and Berries chapter has designs of violets, lilies, pink roses, geraniums and strawberry flowers, plus a stunning centrepiece of spring flowers. Birds and Animals has some charming little pictures – a hare, a group of colourful birds and a parrot picture – plus a superb tiger design that will be a real challenge to work.

If you are looking for a group of pictures for the kitchen or dining room, then the three vegetable and fruit studies are for you. If romance and love tokens are your choice, then the Hearts and Initials chapter has some pretty designs that you can use for greetings cards or simply for sending loving thoughts.

Samplers of all kinds are in a special chapter. For traditionalists, we have designed an alphabet and numbers sampler plus some unusual designs for special gifts. A gardener's sampler, a Christmas sampler and a baby welcome sampler are just three of the designs.

Finally, we have kept some more good things to the last. In the chapter entitled Better Embroidery, we have divulged some of the secrets of working successful embroidery, to help you achieve perfect stitchery. We have tried to make our book a treasure chest of appealing and exciting cross stitch designs. We hope you will have as much fun working them as we had in designing them.

ONE

Flowers and Berries

Autumn hedgerow

This bright sprig of richly-coloured country fruits makes a delightful picture, but it could also be used singly or as a repeating motif on co-ordinated table linen.

Materials

11in (28cm) square of ecru evenweave linen with a thread count of 16 to 1in (2.5cm)

Stranded embroidery cotton as follows: 1 skein each of 2 light beige, 25 oak, 55 Windsor green, 56 viridian green, 60 crimson, 62 bright pink, 80 mid-mauve, 82 dark purple, 107 copper.

Note: Define the straight lines on the chart in back stitch using the shades shown.

Size of finished embroidery: 4½ × 3in (11.5 × 7.5cm)

Preparation

1 Measure and mark the middle of the fabric with basting threads (refer to Better Embroidery).

☐	2
■	25
■	55
■	56
■	60
■	62
■	80
■	82
■	107

Working the embroidery

2 The centre of the chart is indicated by arrows on the edges. This coincides with the basted stitches. Following the chart and the colour key, begin by embroidering the middle block of colour, using 2 strands of thread together. Complete the design as shown on the chart.

Finishing

3 Remove the basting stitches. Press the finished embroidery lightly on the wrong side.

Mounting

4 Mount on cardboard for framing (refer to Better Embroidery).

Before beginning to embroider, it is often useful to tape a short length of each of the thread shades required to a small piece of card, noting its number. This can be invaluable if the thread band becomes detached and lost as the work progresses.

Tiger lilies

These elegant blooms would look superb in any formal setting, perhaps framed and hung in the dining room, or in a gracious bedroom. Adapt the colours to match your decor.

Materials

12in (30cm) square of white evenweave linen with a thread count of 14 threads to 1in (2.5cm)

Stranded embroidery cotton as follows: 1 skein each of 29 pine, 34 orange, 37 mid-yellow, 45 mid-olive green, 53 dark olive green, 100 black

Size of finished embroidery: 5½ × 6in (14 × 15cm)

■	29	■	45
▨	34	■	53
☐	37	■	100

Preparation
1 Measure and mark the middle of the
fabric (see Better Embroidery).

Working the embroidery
2 The centre of the chart is indicated by
arrows on the edges. This coincides with
the basted stitches. Following the chart
and the colour key, begin by

embroidering the middle block of colour,
using 2 strands of thread together.
Complete the design as shown on the
chart.

Finishing
3 Remove the basting stitches. Press the
finished embroidery lightly on the wrong
side and mount for framing.

13

Sweet violets

These delicate blossoms have been captured forever in a spring picture, which would look particularly pretty in a young girl's bedroom. You could also work a set of scatter cushions.

Size of finished embroidery: 5¼ × 5¾in (13 × 15cm)

☐	27	■	43	☐	76	■	81	■ 104
■	42	■	44	■	79	☐	103	

Materials

10 × 12in (25 × 30cm) piece of ecru
  evenweave linen with a thread count of
  16 to 1in (2.5cm)
Stranded embroidery cotton as follows: 1
  skein each of 27 sienna brown, 42 leaf
  green, 43 mid-leaf green, 44 dark leaf
  green, 76 soft pink, 79 dark lavender,
  81 mid-purple, 104 bottle green, 103
  lime green

Preparation

1 Measure and mark the middle of the
fabric (see Better Embroidery).

Working the embroidery

2 The centre of the chart is indicated by
arrows on the edges. This coincides with
the basted stitches. Following the chart
and the colour key, begin by
embroidering the middle block of colour,
using 2 strands of thread together.
Complete the design as shown on the
chart.

Finishing

3 Remove the basting stitches. Press the
finished embroidery lightly on the wrong
side and mount for framing.

A sprig of roses

Besides making a charming picture, this romantic motif could be used, omitting the border, on the corner of a pillow case or repeated along the edge of a crisp white sheet.

Materials

8in (20cm) square of ecru evenweave linen with a thread count of 14 to 1in (2.5cm)

Stranded embroidery cotton as follows: 1 skein each of 49 dark green, 54 dark lime green, 66 dark dusky pink, 69 pale pink, 73 light pink, 75 pink

Size of finished embroidery: 4 × 5in (10 × 12.5cm)

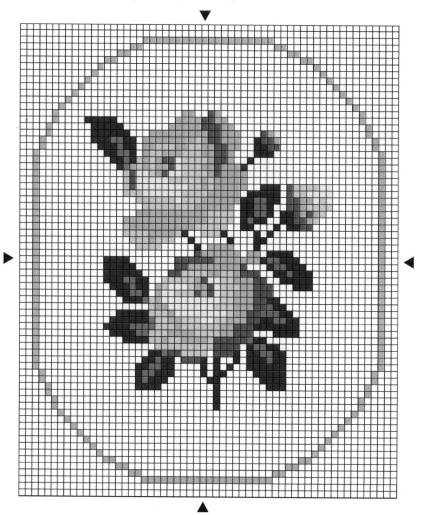

■	49
■	54
■	66
□	69
▨	73
▨	75

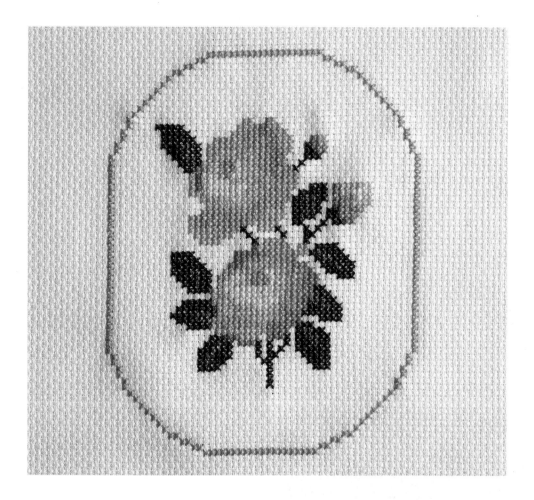

Preparation
1 Measure and mark the middle of the fabric with basting threads (see Better Embroidery).

Working the embroidery
2 The centre of the chart is indicated by arrows on the edges. This coincides with the basted stitches. Following the chart and the colour key, begin by embroidering the middle block of colour, using 2 strands of thread together. Complete the design as shown on the chart.

Finishing
3 Remove the basting stitches. Press the finished embroidery lightly on the wrong side.

Mounting
4 Mount on cardboard for framing (see Better Embroidery).

Try working the design in other colourways, such as yellow and cream for example, to make a pair of stunning pictures for the sitting room or bedroom. On a very fine evenweave fabric this motif would make a delicate design for a diary cover or a box top. You might also try abstracting the lower rose with its leaves for a smaller motif.

A pot of geraniums

Reminiscent of sunny summer days this flower picture will be a cheerful and welcome addition to your kitchen. The colour of the flowers could be changed to peach or pink.

Materials
12 × 10in (30 × 25cm) piece of ecru evenweave linen with a thread count of 14 to 1in (2.5cm)
Stranded embroidery cotton as follows: 1 skein each of 6 stone, 14 chestnut, 15 light chestnut, 19 mid-brown, 45 mid-olive green, 53 dark olive green, 61 pillar box red, 64 mid-red, 100 black

Preparation
1 Measure and mark the middle of the fabric with basting threads (see Better Embroidery).

Working the embroidery
2 The centre of the chart is indicated by arrows on the edges. This coincides with the basted stitches. Following the chart and the colour key, begin by embroidering the middle block of colour, using 2 strands of thread together. Complete the design as shown on the chart.

3 Define the lines on the leaves and the flower pot in back stitch, using 1 strand of shade 100 black. (See Better Embroidery for working back stitch.)

Finishing
4 Remove the basting stitches. Press the finished embroidery lightly on the wrong side.

Mounting
5 Mount the embroidery for framing (see Better Embroidery).

Cross stitch charts can also be used for canvaswork. Why not echo the design of your cross stitch picture in a canvas work cushion which could be worked in either cross or tent stitch.

Size of finished embroidery: 4 × 6in (10 × 15.5cm)

▦	6	■	53
■	14	▦	61
▦	15	▦	64
■	19	■	100
▦	45		

Strawberry circlet

Dainty and delicate, this tiny circlet could be framed to decorate a bedroom, or it could be used in a greetings card to delight a special friend on a birthday.

Materials
9in (23cm) square of ecru evenweave linen with a thread count of 14 to 1in (2.5cm)

Stranded embroidery cotton as follows: 1 skein each of 29 pine, 33 dark orange, 35 light orange, 41 pale leaf green, 45 mid-olive green, 46 light olive green, 53 dark olive green, 61 pillar box red, 100 black

Preparation
1 Measure and mark the middle of the fabric with basting threads (see Better Embroidery).

Size of finished embroidery 2¾in (7cm) square

Working the embroidery
2 The centre of the chart is indicated by arrows on the edges. This coincides with the basted stitches. Following the chart and the colour key, begin by embroidering the middle block of colour, using 2 strands of thread together. Work straight lines in 100 black back stitch. Complete the design as shown on the chart.

Finishing
3 Remove the basting stitches. Press the finished embroidery lightly on the wrong side.

Mounting
4 Mount the embroidery on cardboard for framing (see Better Embroidery).

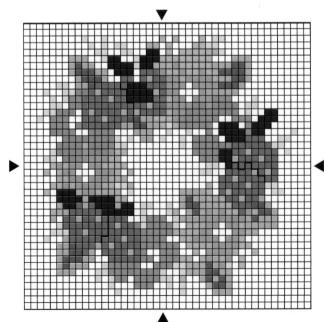

■	29
■	33
■	35
□	41
■	45
■	46
■	53
■	61
■	100

Strawberry pincushion After working the motif, trim the fabric back to a 4in (10cm) square, cut a second piece and sew together. Edge the cushion with a twisted cord.

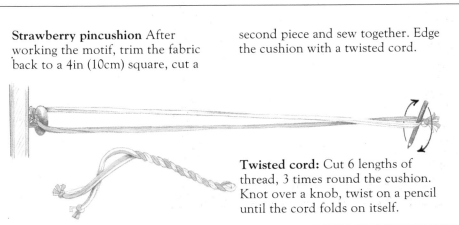

Twisted cord: Cut 6 lengths of thread, 3 times round the cushion. Knot over a knob, twist on a pencil until the cord folds on itself.

Summer nosegay

This bunch of summer flowers is tied with a ribbon and makes a pretty picture for you to frame as a gift. The colours could be changed to blend with any room setting.

Materials
12½in (32cm) square of white evenweave linen with a thread count of 14 to 1in (2.5cm)
Stranded embroidery cotton as follows: 1 skein each of 1 white, 11 mid-salmon, 37 mid-yellow, 43 mid-leaf green, 45 mid-olive green, 47 light hooker green, 49 dark green, 66 dark dusky pink, 69 pale pink, 77 light lavender, 81 mid-purple, 83 dark mauve, 100 black, 118 violet, 120 cream

Preparation
1 Measure and mark the middle of the fabric with basting threads.

Working the embroidery
2 The centre of the chart is indicated by arrows on the edges. This coincides with the basted stitches. Following the chart and the colour key, begin to embroider the middle block of colour, using 2 strands of thread together. Complete the design as shown on the chart.

3 Define the lines between the petals with a single strand of shade 100 black in back stitch. Define the lines of the bow with a strand of shade 66 dark dusky pink in back stitch.

Size of finished embroidery: 6 × 4½in (15 × 11.5cm)

Finishing

4 Remove the basting stitches. Press the finished embroidery lightly on the wrong side and mount on cardboard for framing.

⊡	1	▫	47	■	81
▫	11	■	49	■	83
▫	37	▨	66	■	100
■	43	▫	69	▨	118
■	45	▫	77	▫	120

Blue vase

This striking flower display has the appeal of a Dutch painting. Besides making an imposing picture, it could also be used to stunning effect as a fire screen.

Materials
16 × 14in (40 × 35cm) piece of white evenweave linen with a thread count of 14 to 1in (2.5cm)

Stranded embroidery cotton as follows: 1 skein each of 1 white, 38 yellow, 50 dark hooker green, 52 olive green, 53 dark olive green, 54 dark lime green, 65 cerise, 64 dark cerise, 85 wedgwood blue, 92 dark blue, 95 mid-cobalt blue, 99 charcoal grey, 102 yellow, 109 maroon

When adapting a cross stitch chart for needlepoint take care in choosing your background colour. A dark green, blue or chocolate brown will give a heavy Victorian effect, while soft pinks, peaches and sea greens will blend with a more modern setting. Always buy sufficient skeins of background colour to finish your work, as dye lots can vary considerably.

Preparation
1 Measure and mark the middle of the fabric with basting threads (see Better Embroidery).

Care of embroidered pictures
Embroidered pictures should not be displayed in direct sunlight or under strong artificial lights as these will damage the fabric and cause the colours to fade. Embroideries should be kept away from direct sources of heat, such as radiators or open fires. Dry air, fumes and dust will cause damage, even if the work is framed behind glass. Modern, branded embroidery threads are colour-fast and thus washable. If your embroidery becomes soiled it can be gently squeezed through luke warm suds, rinsed, dried and pressed. Antique textiles should never be washed or dry cleaned without expert advice.

Working the embroidery
2 The centre of the chart is indicated by arrows on the edges. This coincides with the basted stitches. Following the chart and the colour key, begin by embroidering the middle block of colour, using 2 strands of thread together. Complete the design as shown on the chart.

3 Work the petal divisions and the veins on the leaves in back stitch using a single strand of shade 99 charcoal grey. Refer to Better Embroidery for back stitch.

Finishing
4 Remove the basting stitches. Press the finished embroidery lightly on the wrong side.

Mounting
5 Mount the embroidery on cardboard for framing (see Better Embroidery).

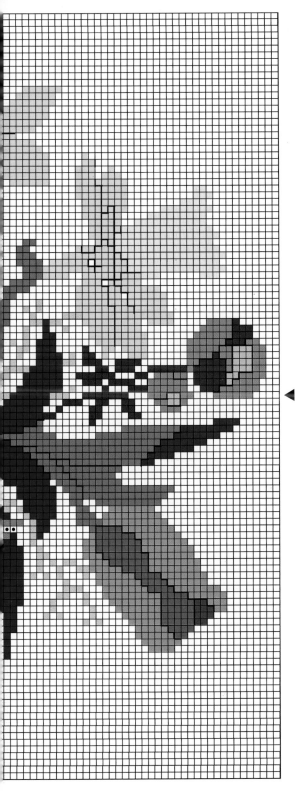

⊡	1
☐	102
■	50
☐	52
■	53
■	54
■	65
■	64
☐	85
■	92
■	95
■	99
☐	38
■	109

Butterfly and flowers

Always a popular subject, a small tortoiseshell butterfly settles on a purple periwinkle flower. The colours could be varied to make a group of three matching pictures.

■ 4	■ 60
■ 24	■ 64
■ 33	■ 79
■ 35	■ 81
■ 53	■ 91
■ 54	■ 100

Materials

12¾in (32cm) square of white evenweave linen with a thread count of 10 to 1in (2.5cm)

Stranded embroidery cotton as follows: 1 skein each of 4 mid-beige, 24 dark oak, 33 dark orange, 35 light orange, 53 dark olive green, 54 dark lime green,

Size of finished embroidery: 6¼ (16cm) square

60 crimson, 64 mid-red, 79 dark
lavender, 81 mid-purple, 91 blue, 100
black

Preparation
1 Measure and mark the middle of the
fabric with basting stitches (see Better
Embroidery).

Working the embroidery
2 The centre of the chart is indicated by
arrows on the edges. This coincides with
the basted stitches. Following the chart
and the colour key, begin by
embroidering the middle block of colour,
using 2 strands of thread together.
Complete the design as shown on the
chart.

Finishing
3 Remove the basting stitches. Press the
finished embroidery lightly on the wrong
side and mount on cardboard for
framing. (Refer to Better Embroidery.)

TWO

Birds and Animals

March hare

A favourite with adults and children alike, this realistic-looking March hare would look charming framed in a dark, rich wood for a hall or perhaps a boy's bedroom.

Materials

12 × 10in (30 × 25cm) piece of ecru evenweave linen with a thread count of 10 to 1in (2.5cm)

Stranded embroidery cotton as follows: 1 skein each of 1 white, 4 mid-beige, 24 dark oak, 100 black, 183 shaded olive green

Size of finished embroidery: 4¼in (11cm) square

◉ 1	■ 24	■ 183
▣ 4	■ 100	

Preparation
1 Measure and mark the middle of the fabric with basting stitches (see Better Embroidery).

Working the embroidery
2 The centre of the chart is indicated by arrows on the edges. This coincides with the basted stitches. Following the chart and the colour key, begin by embroidering the middle block of colour, using 2 strands of thread together. Complete the design as shown on the chart.

3 Define detail on legs, ears and tail in back stitch, using a single strand of shade 100 black.

Finishing
4 Remove the basting stitches. Press the finished embroidery lightly on the wrong side.

Mounting
5 Mount the embroidery on cardboard for framing (see Better Embroidery).

Fabrics and threads
Fine and medium-weight fabrics and embroidery cottons and silks are the most popular materials for cross stitch. However, coarser fabrics and canvas can be worked with soft embroidery cotton and tapestry and crewel wools. Novelty yarns and raffia can also be used for more experimental work. Waste canvas enables you to work cross stitch on plain weave fabrics such as cotton, muslin, cotton lawn and organdie.

Parrot

This bright and cheerful bird design will liven up the kitchen. Besides making a charming picture, the parrot could also be embroidered on accessories such as a coffee pot cover.

Materials

9½ × 10¼in (24 × 26cm) piece of white evenweave linen with a thread count of 14 to 1in (2.5cm)

Stranded embroidery cotton as follows: 1 skein each of 24 dark oak, 40 pear green, 43 mid-leaf green, 60 crimson, 95 mid-cobalt blue, 100 black, 119 off-white

Size of finished embroidery: 3½ × 4¾in (9 × 12cm)

■	24
▨	40
■	43
▨	60
■	95
■	100
□	119

Preparation
1 Measure and mark the middle of the fabric with basting stitches (see Better Embroidery).

Working the embroidery
2 The centre of the chart is indicated by arrows on the edges. This coincides with the basted stitches. Following the chart and the colour key, begin by embroidering the middle block of colour, using 2 strands of thread together.

Complete the design as shown on the chart.

Finishing
3 Remove the basting stitches. Press the finished embroidery lightly on the wrong side.

Mounting
4 Mount the finished embroidery on cardboard for framing (see Better Embroidery).

A flock of birds

These familiar garden birds can be framed individually or mounted together to make a long picture. They could also be used to produce very special greetings cards.

BLUE TIT
Materials
8in (20cm) square of ecru evenweave linen with a thread count of 14 to 1in (2.5cm)

Size of finished embroidery: 4 × 2in (10 × 5cm)

Stranded embroidery cotton as follows: 1 skein each of 1 white, 4 mid-beige, 14 chestnut, 32 dark lemon, 40 pear green, 91 blue, 93 light cobalt blue, 100 black

Note: Define the face and beak in back stitch using a single strand of 100 black.

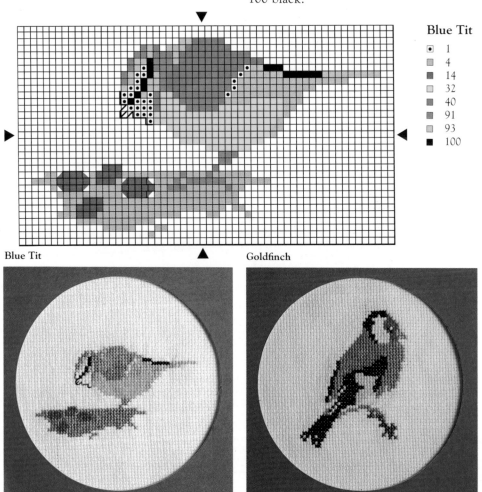

Blue Tit

⊡	1
▨	4
▨	14
☐	32
▨	40
▨	91
☐	93
■	100

Blue Tit   Goldfinch

GOLDFINCH
Materials
8 × 9in (20 × 22cm) piece of ecru
   evenweave linen with a thread count of
   14 to 1in (2.5cm)

Stranded embroidery cotton as follows: 1
skein each of 4 mid-beige, 26 sienna
brown, 37 mid-yellow, 53 dark olive
green, 61 pillar box red, 100 black, 119
off-white, 6 grey

Goldcrest

GOLDCREST
Materials
8in (20cm) square of ecru evenweave
   linen with a thread count of 14 to 1in
   (2.5cm)
Stranded embroidery cotton as follows: 1
   skein each of 6 stone, 15 chestnut, 19
   mid-brown, 32 dark lemon, 39 pale
   yellow, 40 pear green, 45 mid-olive
   green, 100 black, 119 off-white

Goldcrest

☐ 6		■ 45	
■ 15		■ 40	
■ 19		■ 100	
☐ 32		☐ 119	
☐ 39			

Goldfinch

■ 4	☐ 37	■ 100
☐ 6	■ 53	☐ 119
■ 26	■ 61	

Size of finished embroidery: 2½ × 3¼in (6.5 × 8cm)

Size of finished embroidery: 1¾ × 3in (4.5 × 7.5cm)

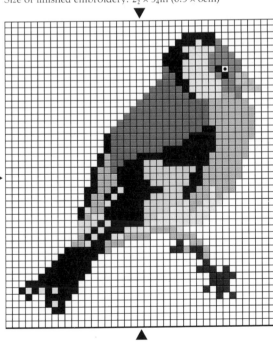

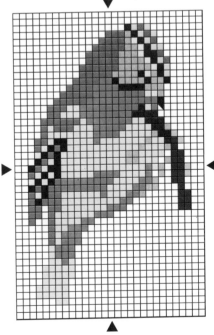

Size of finished embroidery: 3½ × 5in (9 × 12.5cm)

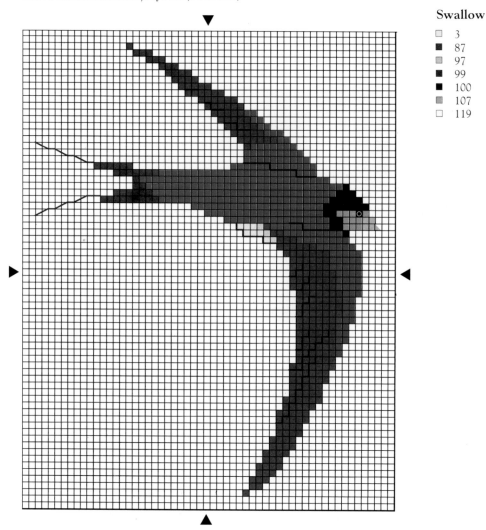

Swallow

☐	3
■	87
▨	97
■	99
■	100
▨	107
☐	119

SWALLOW

Materials

10in (25cm) square of ecru evenweave linen with a thread count of 14 to 1in (2.5cm)

Stranded embroidery cotton as follows: 1 skein each of 3 beige, 87 dark navy blue, 97 light grey, 99 charcoal grey, 100 black, 107 copper, 119 off-white

Note: Define the under-body and tail in back stitch, using a single strand of 100 black.

Preparation

1 Measure and mark the middle of the fabric with basting stitches (see Better Embroidery).

Working the embroidery

2 The centre of each of the charts is indicated by arrows on the edges. This coincides with the basted stitches. Following the charts and the colour keys, begin by embroidering the middle block of colour, using 2 strands of thread together. Complete the designs as shown on the charts.

Swallow

Finishing
3 Remove the basting stitches. Press the finished embroideries lightly on the wrong side.

Mounting
4 If you are mounting the embroideries for a picture, refer to Better Embroidery for the technique.

Bead embroidery
Working on canvas, cross stitch motifs can be adapted to bead embroidery for items such as bags, foot stools and pictures and pincushions. Use half cross stitch to attach the beads to the canvas using 2 strands of thread.

Bear with balloons

A firm favourite with children for many years, no nursery is complete without a teddy bear. This picture could also form the basis of a birthday sampler.

Size of finished embroidery: $4\frac{3}{4} \times 6\frac{3}{4}$in (12 × 17cm)

⊡	1	▨	32
▨	97	■	57
■	26	▨	79
■	24	▨	84
■	14	■	100

Materials

10 × 12in (25 × 30.5cm) piece of ecru evenweave linen with a thread count of 14 to 1in (2.5cm)

Stranded embroidery cotton as follows: 1 skein each of 14 chestnut, 24 dark oak, 26 sienna brown, 32 dark lemon, 57 lime green, 79 dark lavender, 84 light wedgwood blue, 100 black, 1 white, 97 grey.

Note: Define the lines shown on the chart using a single strand of 100 black. Fasten 2 strings of 2 strands of 100 black from the balloons to the bear's paw.

Preparation

1 Measure and mark the middle of the fabric with basting stitches.

Working the embroidery

2 The centre of the chart is indicated by arrows on the edges. This coincides with the basted stitches. Following the chart and the colour key, begin to embroider the middle block of colour, using 2 strands of thread together. Complete the design as shown on the chart.

Finishing

3 Remove the basting stitches. Press the finished embroidery lightly on the wrong side.

Mounting

4 Mount the embroidery on cardboard for framing.

Knitted motifs Cross stitch charts can also be used for knitting, to decorate the front of a sweater with a motif, simply by working each square as a stocking stitch. Alternatively, you can embroider the design directly onto the garment.

Tiger bright

Bold and beautiful, this magnificent picture makes a superb gift for a friend who is interested in the conservation of wildlife. You might also use it to make a calendar.

Materials

12in (30cm) square of ecru evenweave linen with a thread count of 14 to 1in (2.5cm)

Stranded embroidery cotton as follows: 2 skeins of 14 chestnut; 1 skein each of 11 mid-salmon pink, 26 sienna brown, 41 pale leaf green, 45 mid-olive green, 53 dark olive green, 97 light grey, 100 black, 119 off-white, 32 dark lemon

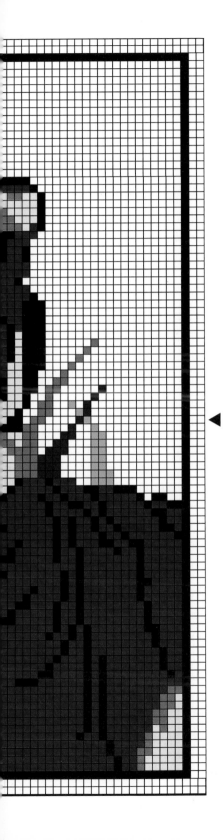

Preparation

1 Measure and mark the middle of the fabric with basting stitches (see Better Embroidery).

Working the embroidery

2 The centre of the chart is indicated by arrows on the edges. This coincides with the basted stitches. Following the chart and the colour key, begin by embroidering the middle block of colour, using 2 strands of thread together. Complete the design. Define the muzzle with black back stitches.

Finishing

3 Remove the basting stitches. Press the finished embroidery lightly on the wrong side.

Mounting

4 Mount the embroidery on cardboard for framing (refer to Better Embroidery).

This tiger motif would look especially striking worked in cross stitch on a black knitted sweater using tapestry wools, 4-ply or double knitting yarn. Work each cross stitch over a knitted stitch. Alternatively, use Swiss embroidery stitches and duplicate the stocking stitches.

☐ 11
■ 14
■ 26
▨ 32
▨ 41
■ 45
■ 53
☐ 97
■ 100
☐ 119

Tabby cat

Everyone's favourite, this tabby cat proudly sits in a field of summer grass. The colours could be changed to produce a cross stitch portrait of your own special feline friend.

Materials
10in (25cm) square of ecru evenweave linen with a thread count of 14 to 1in (2.5cm)

Size of finished embroidery: 4¾in (12cm) square

Stranded embroidery cotton as follows: 1 skein each of 1 white, 40 pear green, 41 pale leaf green, 44 dark leaf green, 45 mid-olive green, 68 light dusky pink, 70 dark pink, 97 light grey, 98 mid-grey, 100 black

⊡	1	☐	68
▦	40	☐	70
▦	41	☐	97
▪	44	▦	98
▦	45	▪	100

Preparation
1 Measure and mark the middle of the fabric with basting stitches (see Better Embroidery).

Working with embroidery
2 The centre of the chart is indicated by arrows on the edges. This coincides with the basted stitches. Following the chart and the colour key, begin by embroidering the middle block of colour, using 2 strands of thread together. Complete the design as shown on the chart.

3 Define the mouth and legs with back stitch (see the straight lines shown on the chart) using a single strand of 100 black.

Finishing
4 Remove the basting stitches. Press the finished embroidery lightly on the wrong side. Mount for framing.

Vegetables and Fruit

Summer's bounty

The three matching pictures in this series could be framed as a single long picture, or individually framed. They would look well framed in a light-coloured wood – pine or maple.

SUMMER SALAD

Materials

12 × 14in (30 × 35cm) piece of white evenweave linen with a thread count of 14 to 1in (2.5cm)

Stranded embroidery cotton as follows: 1 skein each of 1 white, 16 brick red, 20 brown, 21 dark fawn, 43 mid-leaf green, 45 mid-olive green, 46 light olive green, 47 light hooker green, 48 hooker green, 54 dark lime green, 63 dark red, 64 mid-red, 120 cream, 61 pillar box red, 8 dark salmon pink, 100 black

Note: Define the lines on the cucumber in a single strand of 47 light hooker green, using back stitch. Define the lines on the celery stalks and cos lettuce in a single strand of 1 white, using back stitch.

CONTINENTAL VEGETABLES

Materials

12 × 14in (30 × 35cm) piece of white evenweave linen with a thread count of 14 to 1in (2.5cm)

Stranded embroidery cotton as follows: 1 skein each of 3 beige, 4 mid-beige, 5 dark beige, 8 dark salmon pink, 23 light fawn, 37 mid-yellow, 41 pale leaf green, 43 mid-leaf green,

Continental vegetables

☐	3	☐	41	☐	78
☐	4	■	43	◩	80
■	8	■	44	■	81
☐	23	■	45	☐	102
■	5	■	64	☐	120
☐	37	◩	65	■	100
				⊡	1

Size of finished embroidery: 5¾ × 3in (14.5 × 7.5cm)

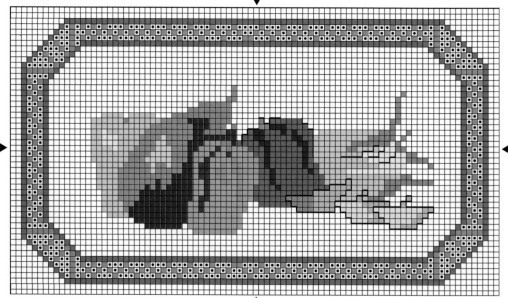

Summer salad

44 dark leaf green, 45 mid-olive green,
64 mid-red, 65 cerise, 78 mid-lavender,
80 mid-mauve, 81 mid-purple,
100 black, 102 yellow, 120 cream,
1 white

Summer salad

⊡ 1	■ 48	
▤ 16	▦ 54	
▦ 20	▦ 63	
▦ 21	▦ 64	
▦ 43	☐ 120	
▦ 45	▦ 61	
▦ 46	▦ 8	
▦ 47	■ 100	

Size of finished embroidery: 5¾ × 3in (14.5 × 7.5cm)

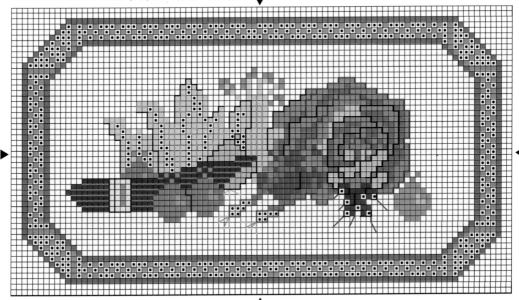

AN ABUNDANCE OF FRUITS
Materials
10 × 12in (25 × 30cm) piece of white
evenweave linen with a thread count of
14 to 1in (2.5cm)

Stranded embroidery cotton as follows: 1
skein each of 2 light beige, 4 mid-beige,
24 dark oak, 33 dark orange, 34
orange, 40 pear green, 43 mid-leaf
green, 45 mid-olive green, 46 light olive
green, 47 light hooker green, 49 dark
green, 51 pale olive green, 52 olive
green, 64 mid-red, 65 cerise, 66 dark
dusky pink, 77 light lavender, 83 dark
mauve, 95 mid-cobalt blue, 100 black,
109 maroon, 120 cream, 176 shaded
pink, 177 shaded strawberry, 31
yellow.

Preparation for all designs
1 Measure and mark the middle of the
fabric pieces with basting stitches (see
Better Embroidery).

Working the embroideries
2 The centre of the charts is indicated by
the arrows on the edges. This coincides
with the basted stitches. Following the
charts and the colour keys, begin by
embroidering the middle block of colour,
using 2 strands of thread together.
Complete the designs as shown on the
charts.

3 Using back stitch and a single strand of
the relevant colour, embroider definition
lines as shown on the charts.

Finishing
4 Remove the basting stitches. Press the
finished embroideries lightly on the
wrong side.

Mounting
5 Mount the embroideries on cardboard
for framing (see Better Embroidery).

Note: The border of An abundance of
fruits has been worked in shades of beige.
If you are working the three pictures as a
set, use white instead of colour 2 beige,
with 4 beige.

An abundance of fruits

An abundance of fruits

▦ 2	▦ 34			▦ 52	
▦ 4	▦ 40	▦ 46		▦ 64	■ 100
■ 24	▦ 43	▦ 47		▦ 65	▦ 109
▦ 33	▦ 45	▦ 49		▦ 66	▦ 120
		▦ 51		▦ 77	▦ 176
				■ 83	▦ 177
				▦ 95	▦ 31

Size of finished embroidery: 5¾ × 3in (14.5 × 7.5cm)

FOUR

Hearts and Initials

Valentine hearts

Embroider your loved one's initial, surrounded by hearts, for a special token on St Valentine's day. This design can be framed for a small picture or it could be put into a greetings card mount.

Materials
10in (25cm) square of ecru evenweave linen with a thread count of 14 to 1in (2.5cm)

Stranded embroidery cotton as follows: 1 skein each of 66 dark dusky pink, 108 red; Twilleys Gold Dust, 1 spool of GD5 silver

Preparation
1 Measure and mark the middle of the fabric with basting stitches (see Better Embroidery).

Size of finished embroidery: 3¾in (9.5cm) square

Working the embroidery
2 The centre of the chart is indicated by the arrows on the edges. This coincides with the basted stitches. Following the chart and the colour key, begin by embroidering the middle block of colour, using 2 strands of thread together. Complete the design as shown on the chart.

Finishing
3 Remove the basting stitches. Press the finished embroidery lightly on the wrong side.

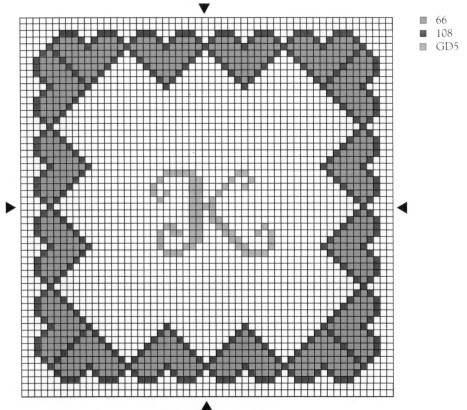

- ▨ 66
- ▪ 108
- ▨ GD5

Mounting

4 Mount the embroidery on cardboard
for framing (see Better Embroidery).

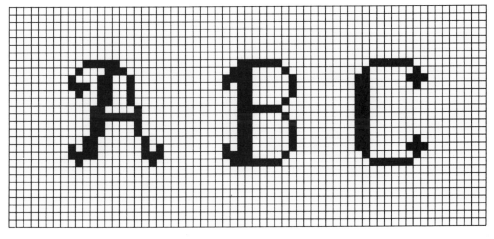

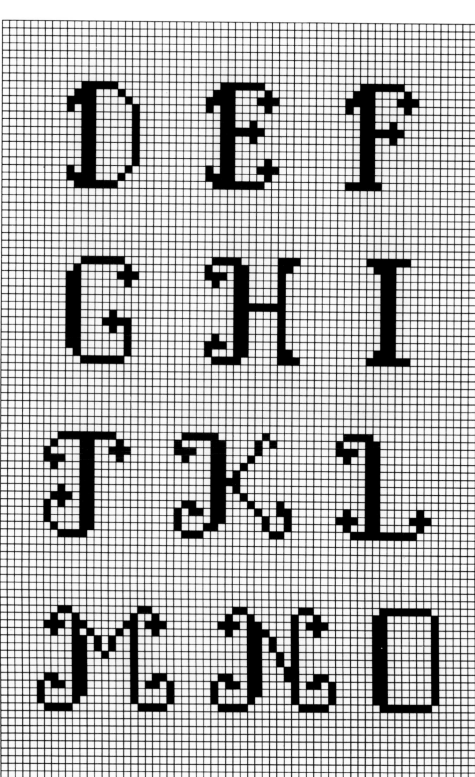

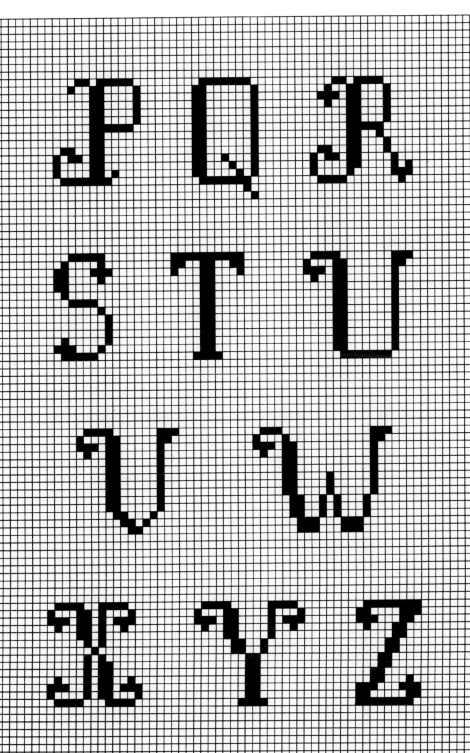

Two hearts as one

Two interlocking hearts embroidered with initials have their own special message. The central motif could also be embroidered on table linens as a wedding gift.

Materials

8 × 11in (20 × 28cm) piece of white evenweave linen with a thread count of 14 to 1in (2.5cm)

Stranded embroidery cotton as follows: 1 skein each of 67 dusky pink, 69 pale pink, 113 turquoise

Preparation

1 Measure and mark the middle of the fabric with basting stitches (see Better Embroidery).

Working the embroidery

2 The centre of the chart is indicated by the arrows on the edges. This coincides with the basted stitches. Following the chart and the colour key, begin by embroidering in the middle of the design, using 2 strands of thread together. Complete the design as shown on the chart.

Finishing

3 Press the finished embroidery lightly on the wrong side.

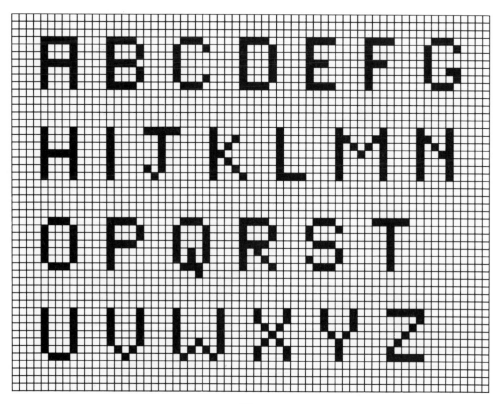

Size of finished embroidery: $2\frac{1}{2} \times 3$in (6 × 7.5cm)

Mounting

4 Mount the embroidery on cardboard for framing or insert it into a greetings card (see Better Embroidery).

■ 113
□ 69
■ 67

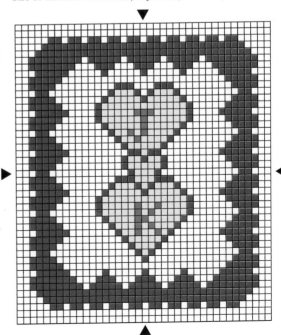

Hearts and roses

This romantic combination of hearts and roses speaks words of love. The dainty border could also be used to decorate a set of towels, the colours changed to match a room.

Materials

9 × 10in (23 × 25cm) piece of white evenweave linen with a thread count of 14 to 1in (2.5cm)

Stranded embroidery cotton as follows: 1 skein each of 42 leaf green, 79 dark lavender, 176 shaded pink.

Preparation

1 Measure and mark the middle of the fabric with basting stitches (see Better Embroidery).

Size of finished embroidery: 3¼ × 4¼in (9 × 10.5cm)

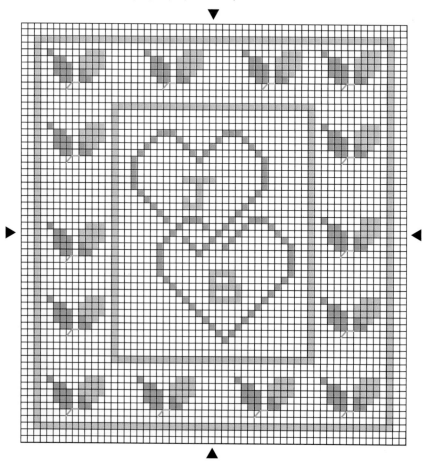

■ 42
■ 79
□ 176

Working the embroidery
2 The centre of the chart is indicated by the arrows on the edges. This coincides with the basted stitches. Following the chart and the colour key, begin by embroidering the middle of the design, using 2 strands of thread together. Complete as shown on the chart.

Finishing
3 Remove the basting stitches. Press the finished embroidery lightly on the wrong side.

Mounting
4 Mount the embroidery on cardboard for framing (see Better Embroidery).

Loving thoughts

Here are two designs that would look equally effective as greetings cards, or mounted and framed as miniatures to express your thoughts in a very special way.

BROKEN HEART
Materials
8in (20cm) square of white evenweave linen with a thread count of 14 to 1in (2.5cm)

Stranded embroidery cotton as follows: 1 skein each of 49 dark green, 64 mid-red, 109 maroon, 117 shaded strawberry

White, square-window card blank

TRUE LOVE
Materials
7in (17.5cm) square of ecru evenweave linen with a thread count of 14 to 1in (2.5cm)

Stranded embroidery cotton as follows: 1 skein of 108 red, Twilleys Gold Dust, 1 spool of GD5 silver

Red, round-window card blank

Preparation
1 Measure and mark the middle of the pieces of fabric with basting stitches (see Better Embroidery).

Working the embroidery
2 The centre of the charts is indicated by arrows on the edges. This coincides with the basted stitches. Following the charts and the colour keys, begin by embroidering the middle block of colour, using 2 strands of thread together. Complete the design as shown on the chart. Work lines in back stitch.

Finishing both cards
3 Remove the basting stitches. Press the finished embroideries lightly on the wrong side.

4 Trim the embroidery edges to fit inside the card, behind the window, leaving as much allowance as possible.

Size of finished embroidery: 2¼ × 2in (5.5 × 5cm)

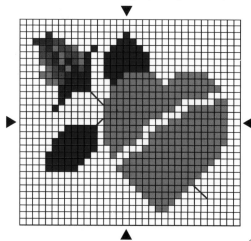

■ 49
■ 64
■ 109
■ 117

Size of finished embroidery: 1⅜ × 1¼in (3.5 × 3cm)

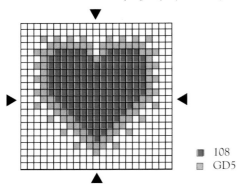

■ 108
□ GD5

5 Spread glue thinly around the edges of the window opening.

6 Stick the embroidery behind the window.

7 Spread a little glue round the edges of the left-hand panel and fold it over the embroidery. Press down firmly and leave until completely dry.

FIVE

Samplers and
Greetings

Alphabet sampler

The traditional sampler of alphabet letters and numbers has been a firm favourite for many years. This version will make a thoughtful gift to record a special occasion.

Materials

16 × 12in (40 × 31cm) piece of ecru evenweave linen with a thread count of 14 to 1in (2.5cm)

Stranded embroidery cotton as follows: 1 skein each of 6 stone, 13 peach, 23 light fawn, 51 pale olive green, 67 dusky pink, 68 light dusky pink, 78 lavender, 79 dark lavender, 93 light cobalt blue, 100 black, 88 mid-petrol blue, 121 dark petrol blue

Preparation

1 Measure and mark the middle of the fabric with basting stitches (see Better Embroidery).

Working the embroidery

2 The centre of the chart is indicated by the arrows on the edges. This coincides with the basted stitches. Following the chart and the colour key, begin by embroidering the middle block of colour, using 2 strands of thread together. Complete the design as shown on the chart.

Finishing

3 Remove the basting stitches. Press the finished embroidery lightly on the wrong side.

Mounting

4 Mount the embroidery on cardboard for framing (see Better Embroidery).

Samplers are very individual embroideries. Unless you are working from a purchased kit, you will probably have an idea of the motifs – and words – you want to include in your sampler. Perhaps the sampler is for a friend who is getting married, or a relative who is moving house. Perhaps someone is an enthusiastic tennis player, and you want to commemorate an important match. Samplers can become a permanent record of every happy occasion, or simply a chance for you to practise your stitchery for your own satisfaction.

Sources of motifs

A selection of motifs is given in Motif Medley which will help you in planning your sampler design. Various alphabets are given in this book, which you can adapt. Alternatively you can work out your own cross stitch motifs.

First, decide on the size of the sampler you wish to make. Choose your fabric, noting the thread count then calculate the number of threads horizontally and vertically to produce a sampler of the required size. Allow for a border and turnings. Having decided on the size of the fabric, mark the area on the graph paper, one square on the paper for every pair of threads on the fabric. Measure and mark the centre of the fabric with basting stitches. Mark the centre of the graph paper area. This gives you working guidelines.

Ideas for the alphabet chart

The chart for an alphabet sampler given here is a simple design and ideal for a beginner. However, it has great potential for designing other more detailed samplers, incorporating motifs and a border. Decide the size of your original sampler first and then plan the border. This can be a single row of stitches or you can work two, or even three, borders, one inside the other. It might look effective to have a row of letters at the top of the sampler – work from this chart. Next, you might like to choose a row of simple flowers from the Motif Medley and work this across the fabric. Perhaps another border, worked across the sampler might come next and then a

Size of finished embroidery: $4\frac{3}{4} \times 10$in (12 × 25cm)

motif or two that particularly characterizes the recipient of your sampler. There are many motifs to choose from – or you might design your own. Refer to Better Embroidery for the technique. Another row of letters and a decorative border strip and your sampler may be complete.

If you want to add a message in small letters, you can use back stitch for this. Work out the words on squared paper first, so that you are sure of setting the words exactly in the centre – or you will find yourself involved in unnecessary unpicking. If you think it suitable, add your name and the date to the bottom area when you have completed the sampler.

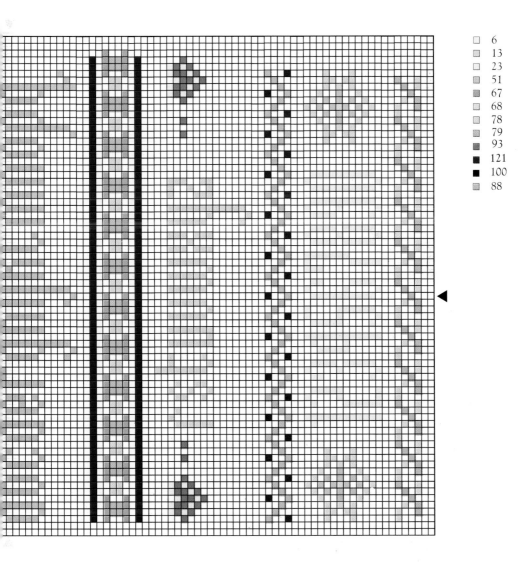

☐	6
☐	13
☐	23
☐	51
☐	67
☐	68
☐	78
☐	79
☐	93
■	121
■	100
☐	88

Decorative borders

A border can make all the difference to an embroidered picture – adopt the colours to match the picture's shades. You can also use these borders when planning a sampler.

If you are using a border pattern on a sampler, this should be carefully charted onto the graph paper first. Begin at the centre of one side of the graph paper shape, colouring in the squares, working towards one corner. To turn the corner, hold a mirror vertically on the graph paper at 45° to the line of the border pattern. This will reflect a symmetrical corner. Copy the corner area, then continue along the second side. Plot each corner in the same way.

When you are including letters or numbers, it is essential to count the number of squares each individual character takes, in depth and width. If suitable letters or numbers are not available as ready-made patterns, trace figures on squared paper, thus making charts of the letters, words or numerals you require. Allow at least one space (stitch) between each letter and four stitches between each word. Work out your letter or word spacing by practising various styles on spare sheets of graph paper, until you are satisfied with the results. They can then be charted onto your design sheet. Spaces between words can be lengthened or shortened to fit the space available and names can be worked in full or with initials and surname. Dates can be in words or numbers.

Small symbols or sections of border pattern can be worked at the ends of short rows of lettering to fill spaces. In old samplers, crowns and hearts were often used for this purpose. A tiny symbol can also be used instead of spacing between words and simple lines of border patterns can be used to divide lines of text.

Decide on the number of squares that

each chosen motif will take, allowing one or more squares for spacing between motifs. Count the number of repeats that can be worked across the fabric. Once you have decided on the number and spacing of your motifs, draw them onto your chart.

A traditional sampler would have included a decorative border, an alphabet, numbers and a suitably uplifting moral or cautionary verse. The initials and name of the needlewoman and either her date of birth or the date on which the sampler was completed might also be added. For a truly authentic effect, remember that an old sampler would not have a mount card within the frame.

Hold the mirror vertically at 45° to the border.

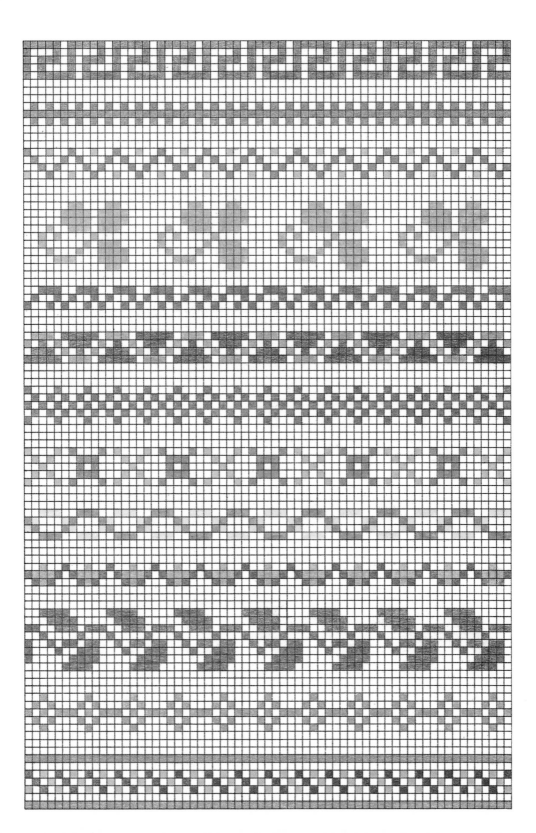

Horseshoes and roses

What better way to mark the happy occasion, than with a personalized wedding sampler of roses and horseshoes? Add the names of the couple and the wedding date.

Materials
16 × 11in (40 × 28cm) piece of white evenweave linen with a thread count of 14 to 1in (2.5cm)
Stranded embroidery cotton as follows: 1 skein each of 43 mid-leaf green, 45 mid-olive green, 68 light dusky pink, 69 pale pink, 70 dark pink, 97 light grey, 99 charcoal grey

Preparation
1 Measure and mark the middle of the fabric with basting stitches (see Better Embroidery).

Working the embroidery
2 The centre of the chart is indicated by the arrows on the edges. This coincides with the basted stitches. Following the chart and the colour key, begin by embroidering the middle block of colour, using 2 strands of thread together. Complete the design as shown on the chart.

Finishing
3 Remove the basting stitches. Press the finished embroidery lightly on the wrong side.

Mounting
4 Mount the embroidery on cardboard for framing (see Better Embroidery).

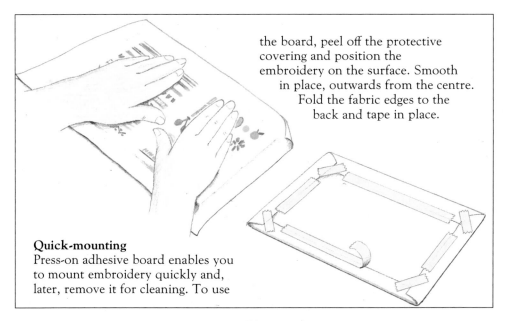

the board, peel off the protective covering and position the embroidery on the surface. Smooth in place, outwards from the centre. Fold the fabric edges to the back and tape in place.

Quick-mounting
Press-on adhesive board enables you to mount embroidery quickly and, later, remove it for cleaning. To use

Size of finished embroidery: 5 × 9in (13 × 22.5cm)

	45		69		97
43		68		70		99

Christmas sampler

Make this festive sampler to become part of your Christmas traditions. You could also abstract a motif for a bright border of Christmas trees on a seasonal tablecloth and table napkins.

⊡	1
■	24
▨	33
▨	43
▨	50
▨	60
▨	73
▨	80
▨	85
▨	86
▨	97
■	100
▨	102

Materials

12 × 14in (30 × 35cm) piece of ecru evenweave linen with a thread count of 14 to 1in (2.5cm)

Stranded embroidery cotton as follows: 1 skein each of 1 white, 24 dark oak, 33 dark orange, 43 mid-leaf green, 50 dark hooker green, 60 crimson, 73 light pink, 80 mid-mauve, 85 wedgwood blue, 86 French navy, 97 light grey, 100 black, 102 yellow

Preparation

1 Measure and mark the middle of the fabric with basting stitches (see Better Embroidery).

Working the embroidery

2 The centre of the chart is indicated by the arrows on the edges. This coincides with the basted stitches. Following the chart and the colour key, begin by embroidering the middle block of colour, using 2 strands of thread together. Complete the design as shown on the chart.

Finishing

3 Remove the basting stitches. Press the embroidery lightly on the wrong side.

Mounting

4 Mount the embroidery on cardboard for framing (see Better Embroidery).

Waste canvas

When cross stitch is to be worked on a plain weave fabric – such as when decorating handkerchiefs, bedlinens, lingerie or children's clothes etc – waste canvas is used over the ground fabric to provide a guide for the stitches. Waste canvas can be purchased at most needlework counters but ordinary embroidery canvas can be used as long as the threads are not interlocked.

Baste the waste canvas into position on the fabric to be embroidered. Work the design, taking the cross stitches through the waste canvas and onto the fabric beneath, using the canvas threads to position the cross stitches.

When the embroidery is completed, dampen the embroidery with water until the canvas threads begin to soften and part. Gently withdraw the canvas threads, first the vertical then the horizontal. Remove the basting threads. It is important to match the canvas mesh to the ground fabric. A fine fabric will need a canvas with 14 or 16 mesh while a coarser ground fabric will need a mesh of 12 to 1in (2.5cm) or less.

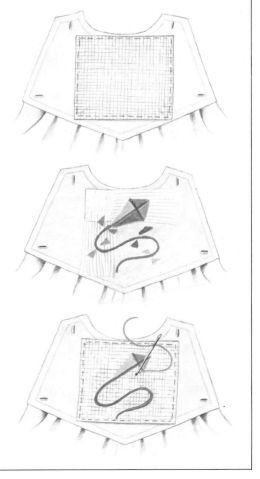

Christmas cards

Embroidered greetings cards are fun to make, taking only a few hours to complete – but they'll be treasured by friends and family for years to come.

CHRISTMAS STOCKING
Materials
4 × 6in (10 × 15cm) piece of white evenweave linen with a thread count of 14 to 1in (2.5cm)

Stranded embroidery cotton as follows: 1 skein each of 54 dark lime green, 64 red, 81 mid-purple, 75 pink, 93 light cobalt blue, 100 black, 119 off-white

White greetings card blank with a rectangular window

Note: Define the stocking and parcels in back stitch, using a single strand of 100 black.

CHRISTMAS CANDLE
Materials
4 × 5in (10 × 12.5cm) piece of white evenweave linen with a thread count of 14 to 1in (2.5cm)

Stranded embroidery cotton as follows: 1 skein each of 34 orange, 38 yellow, 40 pear green, 43 mid-leaf green, 49 dark green, 54 dark lime green, 59 mid-crimson, 69 pale pink, 99 charcoal grey, 107 copper

White greetings card blank with an oval window

Note: Outline the candle flame in back stitch, using a single strand of 99 charcoal grey.

Preparation
1 Measure and mark the middle of the fabric with basting stitches (see Better Embroidery).

Working the embroidery
2 The centre of the chart is indicated by arrows on the edges. This coincides with the basted stitches. Following the chart and colour key, begin by embroidering the middle block of colour, using 2 strands of thread together. Complete the design as shown on the chart.

Finishing
3 Remove the basting stitches. Press the finished embroidery lightly on the wrong side.

4 Trim the edges of the fabric to fit the card, leaving as much allowance as possible around the actual embroidery.

5 Spread glue thinly around the edges of the window.

6 Stick the embroidery behind the window.

7 Spread glue round the edges of the left hand panel and fold over the embroidery. Press down firmly and leave to dry thoroughly.

Size of finished embroidery: $2 \times 2\frac{1}{2}$in (5×6cm)

Size of finished embroidery: $1\frac{1}{2} \times 2\frac{1}{2}$in ($4 \times 6$cm)

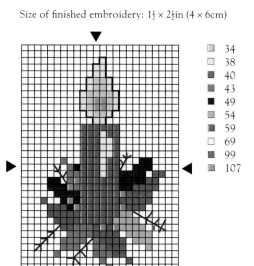

	34
	38
	40
	43
	49
	54
	59
	69
	99
	107

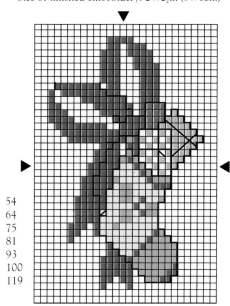

	54
	64
	75
	81
	93
	100
	119

Welcome to baby

This charming baby sampler, can be worked with the alphabet or with the baby's name and date of birth. Use the motif to decorate a cot cover as well.

Materials
11in (28cm) square of white evenweave linen with a thread count of 14 to 1in (2.5cm)
Stranded embroidery cotton as follows: 1 skein each of 1 white, 26 sienna brown, 47 light hooker green, 79 dark lavender, 100 black, 24 dark oak; you will also need 1 skein of 11 mid-salmon and 69 pale pink for a girl or 85 wedgwood blue and 84 light wedgwood blue for a boy

Preparation
1 Measure and mark the middle of the fabric with basting stitches (see Better Embroidery).

Working the embroidery
2 The centre of the chart is indicated by the arrows on the edge. This coincides with the basted stitches. Following the chart and the colour key, begin by embroidering the middle block of colour, using 2 strands of thread together. Complete the design as shown in the chart.

Finishing
3 Remove the basting stitches. Press the finished embroidery lightly on the wrong side.

4 Embroider trimmings on the crib in either 11 mid-salmon and 69 pale pink (for a girl) or 85 wedgwood blue and 84 light wedgwood blue (for a boy). Outline the crib, teddy and cushion in a single strand of 99 charcoal grey in back stitch.

Mounting
5 Mount the embroidery on cardboard for framing (see Better Embroidery).

The crib motif could also be used on a variety of nursery accessories, using the waste canvas method

Size of finished embroidery: 6 × 7¼in (15 × 18cm)

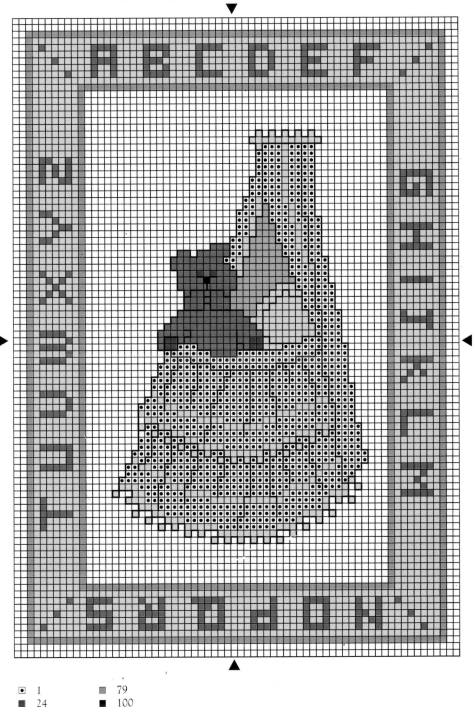

▫	1	▪	79
▪	24	■	100
▪	47	▫	11
▪	26	▫	69

Gardener's sampler

Here is a colourful picture that makes a perfect gift for a gardening friend. The border could also be embroidered on the pocket or along the hem of a gardening apron.

Materials

$12\frac{1}{2} \times 10\frac{1}{2}$in (31 × 26cm) piece of white evenweave linen with a thread count of 14 to 1in (2.5cm)

Stranded embroidery cotton as follows: 1 skein each of 1 white, 4 mid-beige, 14 chestnut, 15 light chestnut, 19 mid-brown, 24 dark oak, 33 dark orange, 35 light orange, 43 mid-leaf green, 46 light olive green, 49 dark green, 59 mid-crimson, 61 pillar box red, 79 dark lavender, 82 dark purple, 97 light grey, 99 charcoal grey

☐ 4	▨ 33	▨ 61
■ 14	☐ 35	☐ 79
☐ 15	■ 43	■ 82
■ 19	☐ 46	☐ 97
■ 24	■ 49	■ 99
	▨ 59	

Size of finished embroidery: 6 × $4\frac{1}{4}$ (15 × 10.5cm)

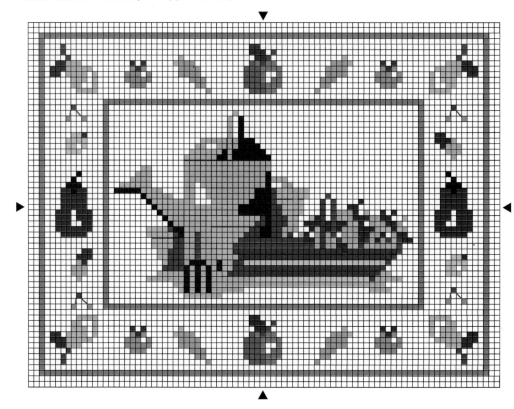

Preparation
1 Measure and mark the middle of the fabric with basting stitches (see Better Embroidery).

Working the embroidery
2 The centre of the chart is indicated by the arrows on the edges. This coincides with the basted stitches. Following the chart and the colour key, begin by embroidering the middle block of colour, using 2 strands of thread together. Complete the design as shown.

3 Define the watering can with 99 charcoal back stitch. Work the highlights on the fruits and vegetables in the border and the watering can in 1 white.

Finishing
4 Remove the basting stitches. Press the finished embroidery lightly on the wrong side.

Mounting
5 Mount the embroidery on cardboard for framing (see Better Embroidery).

Home, sweet home

This picture of a little country cottage would make a treasured addition to any home. Names and a date could be substituted for the alphabet to provide a unique house-warming gift.

Materials
12 × 10in (30 × 25cm) piece of white evenweave linen with a thread count of 14 to 1in (2.5cm)
Stranded embroidery cotton as follows: 1 skein each of 3 beige, 17 rust, 18 dark brown, 24 dark oak, 43 mid-leaf green, 48 hooker green, 54 dark lime green, 60 crimson, 97 light grey, 100 black, 104 bottle green, 1 white

Size of finished embroidery: 6 × 5in (15 × 12.5cm)

Preparation
1 Measure and mark the middle of the fabric with basting stitches (see Better Embroidery).

Working the embroidery
2 The centre of the chart is indicated by the arrows on the edges. This coincides with the basted stitches. Following the chart and the colour key, begin by embroidering the middle block of colour, using 2 strands of thread together. Complete the design as shown in the chart.

▢	3	▢	54
■	17	■	60
■	18	▢	97
■	24	■	100
■	43	■	104
■	48	▣	1

Finishing
3 Remove the basting stitches. Press the finished embroidery lightly on the wrong side.

Mounting
4 Mount the embroidery on cardboard for framing (see Better Embroidery).

USING FLEXI-FRAMES
Flexi-frames consist of two rings, an inner of rigid plastic and an outer of flexible plastic. Fabric is fitted between the two rings and afterwards, the flexi-frame can be used as a picture frame. Remove the finished embroidery from the frame. Place the rigid frame on the wrong side and trace round. Gather the edges, pull up the stitches and replace the embroidery in the flexi-hoop. Trim the excess fabric on the wrong side.

Greeting for a special friend

This pretty frame could contain a friend's initials, a date to mark a special occasion or, as here, simply a nosegay of blossoms.

Materials
11in (28cm) square of white evenweave
   linen with a thread count of 14 to 1in
   (2.5cm)
Stranded embroidery cotton as follows: 1
   skein each of 51 pale olive green, 69
   pale pink, 75 pink, 79 dark lavender,
   84 light wedgwood blue

Size of finished embroidery: 4¼ (10.25cm) square

Preparation
1 Measure and mark the middle of the
fabric with basting stitches (see Better
Embroidery).

■	51
□	69
▨	75
■	79
▨	84

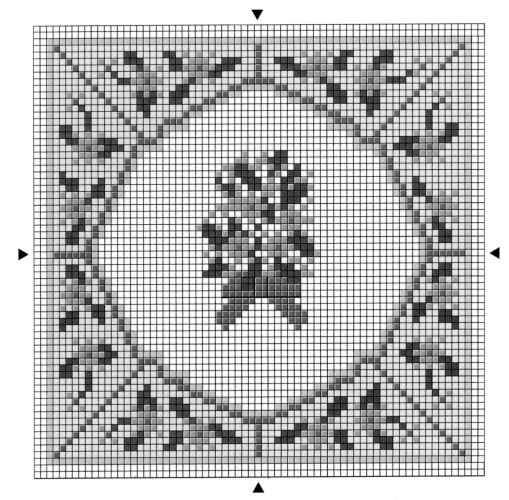

Working the embroidery

2 The centre of the chart is indicated by the arrows on the edges. This coincides with the basted stitches. Following the chart and the colour key, begin by embroidering the middle block of colour, using 2 strands of thread together. Complete as shown in the chart.

Finishing

3 Remove the basting stitches. Press the finished embroidery lightly on the wrong side.

Mounting

4 Mount the embroidery on cardboard for framing (see Better Embroidery).

Clown picture

This happy clown picture would make the perfect birthday present. Worked on canvas, the design is also suitable for a needlepoint cushion or a needlemade rug, using tapisserie wools or rug wool.

Materials
12in (30cm) square of white evenweave linen with a thread count of 12 to 1in (2.5cm)

Stranded embroidery cotton as follows: 1 skein each of 61 pillar box red, 42 leaf green, 33 orange, 36 yellow, 1 white, 100 black, 86 French navy

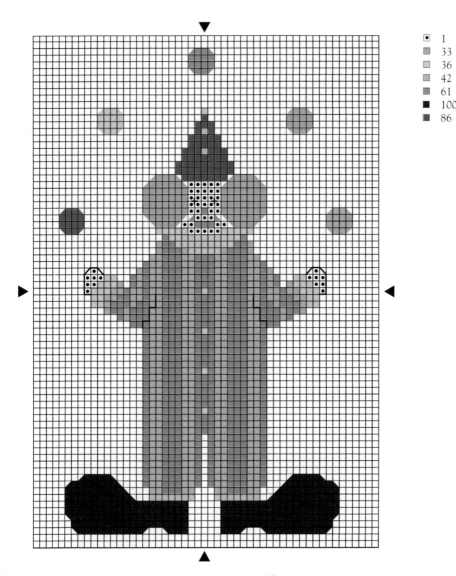

⊡	1
▨	33
▢	36
▨	42
▨	61
■	100
■	86

Preparation
1 Measure and mark the middle of the fabric with basting stitches (see Better Embroidery).

Working the embroidery
2 The centre of the chart is indicated by the arrows on the edges. This coincides with the basted stitches. Following the chart and the colour key, begin by embroidering the middle block of colour, using 2 strands of thread together. Complete the design as shown on the chart.

3 Using back stitch and a single strand of the relevant colour, embroider the definition lines as shown on the chart.

Finishing
4 Remove the basting stitches. Press the finished embroidery lightly on the wrong side.

Mounting
5 Mount the embroidery on cardboard for framing (see Better Embroidery). Size of finished embroidery $6\frac{5}{8} \times 4$in (17 × 10cm).

Motif medley

Use these motifs to create your own samplers or to personalize clothing, household linen and soft furnishings. They are also ideal for making special greetings cards.

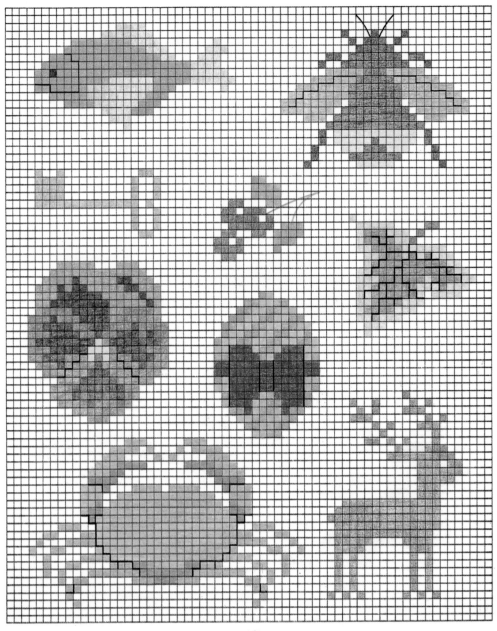

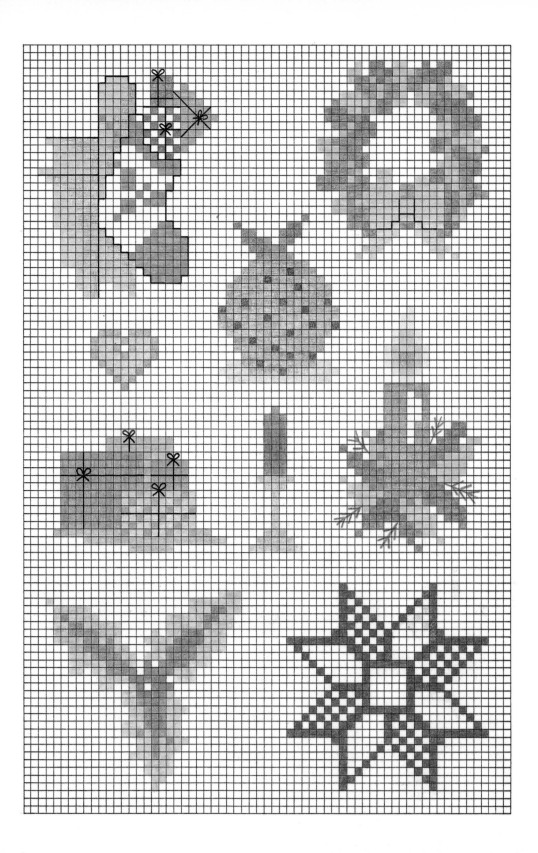

SIX

Better Embroidery

❧

In this chapter you will find advice and tips on all aspects of embroidery – from choosing threads and fabrics and setting up your frame to charting your own cross stitch designs.

BASIC TOOLS AND EQUIPMENT

Very little basic equipment is required to enable you to produce stunning cross stitch pictures. This chapter will give advice on choosing the right tools for the projects shown in this book.

Scissors

For cutting fabric to the correct size, sharp dressmaker's scissors will be required, while for general embroidery a pair of fine, pointed and very sharp embroidery scissors is essential.

Always keep your scissors for the purpose for which they were designed. Cutting paper will quickly blunt the blades. Never use unpicking tools for embroidery work as these can accidentally rip the ground threads of the fabric.

Needles

Round-ended tapestry needles are most suitable for working on evenweave fabrics. These will pass easily through the holes in the fabric, without snagging or splitting the threads. Split threads will result in distorted stitches, which will not lie correctly. Tapestry needles are available in sizes from 13 to 26. Chenille needles (sizes 13–24) are sharp-pointed with large eyes. Use these for general embroidery using heavier threads. Crewel needles (sizes 1–10) are also sharp with large eyes. Choose these for general, surface embroidery.

For basting and finishing projects, a range of sharps sewing needles will be required.

Needles should never be left in the fabric. They can cause the threads to distort and may leave a permanent stain.

Pins

Always use stainless steel pins for your work. Discard any that are bent or rusty and never leave pins in fabric for too long, as this can leave marks which will be difficult to remove. Glass-headed pins (which are manufactured from broken needles) are recommended. They are both strong and sharp.

Measuring aids

An accurate tape measure or ruler is essential for measuring and cutting fabric. When buying a new measure, make sure it shows both inches and centimetres and remember that cloth measuring tapes stretch with use. Check your tape measure against a ruler to ensure that the measurements are still accurate and replace it if necessary.

Thimbles

Many people find it helpful to work with a thimble. However, if you are not one of these, a piece of sticking plaster over the middle finger can help to prevent soreness that can be caused by the end of the needle.

THREADS AND YARNS

Most needlework shops stock a wide range of colours and types of thread. Choose the type suited to the kind of embroidery you are working and the effect you wish to achieve.

Stranded cotton

This is formed from six strands loosely twisted together. These strands can be separated and used individually for finer work or used in different combinations. As a general guide, on 10 to 16 count fabric use 2 or 3 strands; on 16 to 24 count use 2 strands and on 24 to 36 count use 1 strand. Stranded cotton works well in most types of embroidery.

Danish flower thread

This is a matte-finish thread made of combed cotton. On counts of 14 to 20 use 2 threads, on counts of 20 or more use 1 thread.

Soft embroidery cotton (coton à broder)

This is a dull-surfaced 5-ply thread, usually used on heavier fabrics.

Perlé (pearl) cotton

This is a glossy, twisted 2-ply thread which comes in three thicknesses. It is ideal for embroidery on coarse (low count) fabrics.

Pure silk

These four-strand threads have a high gloss sheen and come in a wonderful range of jewel-bright colours. Silk threads are colour-fast up to 60° and should be pressed with a cool iron. Silk threads are suitable for most kinds of fine embroidery.

Crewel wool

A fine, 2-ply, wool, this is used both in fine canvas embroidery and for surface stitchery on fabric.

Tapestry wool

This is a tightly twisted 4-ply yarn. It is available in a wide range of colours and is colour-fast. Usually used for canvaswork, tapestry wool can be divided into single strands for other types of embroidery.

FABRICS

Evenweave fabric

This is the most popular fabric for cross stitch. It is so named because the number of warp and weft threads in a measured inch (2.5cm) is exactly the same. It can be obtained in a variety of sizes (thread counts) types and a range of pale colours. The highest number thread count denotes the finest weave and will, therefore, produce the smallest stitches. Fabrics range from 10 threads to the inch (2.5cm) to 36 threads to the inch (2.5cm).

Hardanger is a type of evenweave fabric in which the pairs of threads are woven together. This fabric is ideal for counted thread techniques, including cross stitch and blackwork embroidery, as the threads are easily counted and the embroidery remains firm during use.

Aida is an evenweave fabric in which the warp and weft threads have been grouped together. This creates clearly defined holes through which the needle can pass.

Binca or Bincarette is the name given to evenweave fabric with a count of 10 threads to 1in (2.5cm). Cross stitch worked on this is large and bold and is, therefore, suitable for children who are learning embroidery.

Plain weave fabrics

These do not have the characteristics of evenweave, but some types can be used for counted thread embroidery. Generally, plain weave fabrics have a smooth, tightly woven surface and the number of threads in the warp and weft are not always the same. This category includes cotton, cotton and polyester mixes, muslin, organdie, fine embroidery linen and speciality fabrics such as hessian and hopsacking. Plain weave is most suitable for surface, free-style embroidery.

PREPARING FABRIC

If the fabric is creased in any way, particularly along the centre fold line, it is advisable to steam-iron thoroughly before cutting or beginning to embroider. Evenweave fabric tends to fray on cut edges, so either turn and baste a hem or bind the fabric edges with masking tape.

Before starting to embroider, the exact middle of the fabric must be located by carefully counting the threads along one side, then along the adjacent side to find the centres. Mark the half-way points with pins then with lines of coloured basting thread running from top to bottom and then across.

Where the two lines of threads cross is the centre point. When working with a very fine fabric, measure and mark the middle of the sides with pins then work lines of basting stitches between the pins.

Work basting stitches top to bottom, then across.

Some embroidery fabrics are given a finishing dressing before they leave the manufacturer. This can make them feel fairly stiff to handle. You may want to wash this away before beginning to embroider, although the stiffness of the fabric can help to give your work an even tension.

EMBROIDERY FRAMES

In order to produce even, high quality cross stitch, it is essential to work with a frame. A correctly framed evenweave fabric enables the needleworker to work neatly and smoothly and the finished results will more than justify the time and initial effort required.

Experience will show which frame is best suited to a particular piece of work, but, in general, small motifs are most quickly and easily worked in a round, tambour frame, while larger, more elaborate pieces are better in rectangular or slate frames.

Stretcher frames are simply four pieces of wood joined at the corners. To attach the fabric, mark the middle of each side of the frame. Mark the centre of the fabric with basting stitches. Line up the marks and fix the fabric with staples or drawing pins. Old picture frames can also be used as a kind of stretcher frame.

Tambour or ring frames

A tambour frame consists of two rings, the outer of which has a screw fitting. This is tightened to enable the ring to hold the fabric firmly in place. Frames can be made of wood or plastic.

Tambour frames are available in several sizes from tiny, 4in (10cm) diameter embroidery rings to large quilting hoops of 15in (38cm) diameter.

Framing up tambour frames
1 Separate the two rings of the frame. Place the fabric to be embroidered over the smaller ring and fit the larger ring over this, making sure that the marked centre is in the middle of the frame.
2 Smooth the fabric out evenly and straighten the grain as you tighten the tension screw. As you continue to tighten the outer ring, pull the fabric gently from time to time to obtain an even and firm surface.

Pull the fabric edges gently for an even surface.

When working with slippery or delicate fabrics, it is advisable to bind the smaller ring with thin, cotton tape before assembling. This will help to hold the fabric more firmly and prevents damage to fine fabric.

At the end of each session, loosen the screw and remove the larger ring. Cover the worked embroidery with tissue to protect it. Replace the ring without screwing down tightly. At the next session, tighten the screw then tear the paper away over the embroidery.

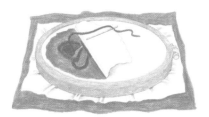

Protect partly-worked embroidery with tissue.

Rotating frames
These frames are composed of two top rollers or bars, with tapes attached, and two side sections. The rollers slot into the side pieces and are held securely by pegs or butterfly screw attachments. The tape length regulates the size of these frames and they vary from 12in (30cm) to 27in (68cm).

Framing up rotating frames
It is essential to allow at least an extra 1in (2.5cm) on all sides when buying or cutting the fabric. Baste a single hem on the top and bottom edges of the fabric. Oversew 1in (2.5cm)-wide strong tape down each side.

Working from the centre outwards, oversew the top and bottom hemmed edges to the roller tapes, using a strong thread and small stitches. Fit the rollers into the side pieces. Turn the rollers until the fabric is taut. Tighten the butterfly screws (or insert the pegs).

Thread a darning needle with strong thread and firmly lace the side edges to the side pieces. Oversew several times at each end to secure, wrapping the thread around the rollers before finishing. Tighten the lacings occasionally as you work. Slacken off the lacings between sessions.

Embroidery rings are useful when working small areas of embroidery, as a very tiny piece of fabric can be stitched onto a larger calico square before stretching it in the frame. Once the frame is set up, the calico behind the fabric area to be embroidered is cut away carefully, using fine, sharp scissors.

MAKING A START

If working cross stitch for the first time, choose a design that is not too complex. A small design with only a few colours is best. Work with good quality fabric and colour-fast threads.

It is advisable to work in a comfortable chair in a good light. This is particularly important when using higher count fabrics and several shades of colour. An overhead lamp is useful, particularly if it is fitted with a daylight simulation bulb. This will reduce eye strain and allow the correct colour matching of threads.

The best cross stitch embroidery has clearly defined stitches that cover the ground fabric well and look crisp and sharp. If the thread begins to fray while working, do not continue. Finish the thread off neatly and begin again.

To begin, cut a length of stranded yarn approximately 12in (30cm) and divide this into separate strands. Smooth each strand between finger and thumb before regrouping and threading the needle. Do not tie a knot in the end, as this will make the finished work lumpy. Pull the needle through from the front of the fabric, leaving a tail of about 2in (5cm) on the right side. Hold this tail securely while the first stitch is worked. When several stitches are completed, the tail can be threaded onto a needle and taken through to the back of the work and then woven through the back of worked stitches.

Working cross stitch
Cross stitch can be worked in rows from right to left or left to right, over any number of threads.
1 Bring the needle through at 1, insert diagonally at 2, bring out again above at 3. Insert again at 4 to make the next slanting stitch.
2 To complete the cross, work back in the opposite direction. From 3, go diagonally down to 4 and out at 5.

Working diagonally
1 Bring the needle through at 1, go diagonally down to 2, across to 3, insert at 4, come out at 5.
2 From 5, go diagonally down to 1 and out at 2.
3 Go diagonally up to 4 and out at 5. Continue.

Half cross stitches
Sometimes, single diagonal stitches are used on the edge of a design to achieve a rounded edge. Where this is required, diagonal lines, usually in the thread colour required, are printed across the pattern squares.

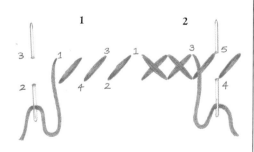

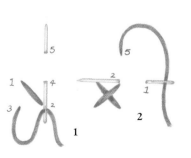

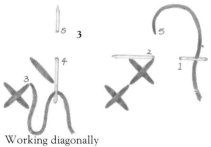

Working diagonally

101

When working surface embroidery, insert the needle on the right side a little way from the stitching, leaving a short tail. Work the embroidered area and finish off with a few small straight stitches. Draw the tail of thread through to the back of the work and darn in. Make sure that the finishing stitches are as flat as possible and not too close together. Snip away any excess threads.

Blocks of colour
To embroider a block of cross stitches in one colour, first work a row of half cross stitches, either horizontally or vertically. When the row is completed, work in the reverse direction completing the cross. Always work the top stitch of each cross stitch in the same direction on any piece of embroidery.

Scattered stitches
If stitches of one colour are scattered in small groups on the chart, do not fasten the thread off after each block, but take the thread through to the reverse of the fabric and secure, with the needle, away from the area being worked. Using another needle, continue to follow the chart until the first colour is required again. This method should only be used when working in a small area, otherwise the fabric may become puckered.

Large areas
When covering a large area, it is advisable to work in horizontal rows. The first diagonal of each stitch should be completed from right to left. Then, by working back along this row from left to right, the cross stitches will be formed. Continue to build the colour block by working each successive row in this way.

Working diagonally
To work diagonal lines of cross stitches work downwards or upwards and completing each complete cross before beginning the next.

Filling shapes
When filling a shape with colour, begin to embroider across its widest point. Try to bring the needle up through unworked fabric and down through holes where stitches have already been worked.

FOLLOWING A CHART
The cross stitch designs in this book are all worked from graphed charts, in which each coloured square represents one cross stitch. A colour key is given with each chart for identifying the embroidery thread numbers.

The centre of the chart is indicated by the arrows at its edges. This coincides with the basting stitches worked to mark the middle of the fabric. The instructions given with each project tell you to begin working the embroidery from the middle of the design.

Check list
Here is your check list for working and framing cross stitch pictures.

Evenweave fabrics
Crewel needles
Sewing needles
Stranded embroidery cotton
Basting thread
Embroidery scissors
Dressmakers' scissors
Tape measure
Tambour hoop
Tissue paper
Embroidery pencils
Soft drawing pencils
Squared graph paper
Coloured pencils
Clear acetate grids
Pins
Crafts knife
Metal rule
Self-adhesive mounting boards
Adhesive tape, masking tape
Mounting card
Button thread
Lacing needle

EMBROIDERY STITCHES

There are literally hundreds of embroidery stitches to choose from when you are decorating fabric. Here are some of the most popular.

Satin stitch

This is used for filling shapes. Work stitches evenly and laid so that they touch. Bring the needle through at A, insert it at B and bring it through again at C.

Straight stitch

Straight stitches are one of the simplest stitches and used individually or to build up designs, like this eight-point star. Bring the needle through at A, insert it at B and bring it through again at C.

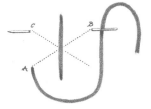

Back stitch

This stitch is used often in this book, usually to define a design line. It can be worked in straight lines or in curves. Bring the needle through at A, insert it at B and bring it out at C in front of A.

Stem stitch

As the name suggests this stitch is often used to indicate stems. Bring the needle through at A, the thread below the needle. Insert it at B and bring it through again at C.

Chain stitch

To work this stitch, bring the needle through at A and, with the thread below the needle, insert it beside A at B. The thread forms a loop. Bring the needle through at C, pull through gently, ready to start the next chain stitch.

French knot

French knots are used single or massed in groups. Bring the needle through at A, wind the thread round the needle twice and then insert the point at B, close by A. Pull the thread through so that the knot tightens on the fabric surface.

FINISHING

Remove the embroidery from its frame. Snip and pull out any basting stitches. Snip off any stray threads from the back of the work wherever possible, but be careful not to cut too close to your stitching. Remove masking tape from the fabric edges if it has been used.

Press the work lightly on the wrong side, using a steam iron to smooth the fabric and 'emboss' the stitches.

If you are storing the finished embroidery, do not fold it. Store it flat in white, acid-free tissue paper.

FRAMING EMBROIDERY PICTURES

Consideration should be given to whether to frame the embroidery yourself or to take it to a professional. It should, however, be delivered for framing ready mounted on card. The type of frame should be carefully chosen and any framer familiar with framing textiles should be able to advise on this. Very fine work should be mounted behind glass to protect from dust and atmospheric pollution, but raised embroidery will be flattened and should be left unglazed. The most important consideration is that the glass should not touch the embroidery. A special spray can be used to give some protection to work framed without glass. Unglazed pictures can be given a slightly padded look, by inserting a layer of wadding between the embroidery and the cardboard mount.

It is possible to purchase non-reflective glass for framing, but this tends to alter the colours in the work very slightly, as it has a grey tinge.

MOUNTING EMBROIDERY

To prepare embroidery for framing, cut a sheet of white mounting card to the size of the frame rebate. Trim the embroidery fabric back to 2in (5cm) all round. Centre the embroidery on the card, right side up. Fold the top and bottom edges over to the back, then fold the side edges over. Push pins into the edges of the card to hold the fabric in place. Gently pull the fabric taut as you pin, so that the embroidery lies smooth and taut.

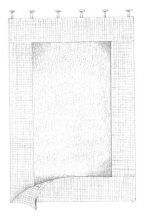

Fold the edges to the back and pin.

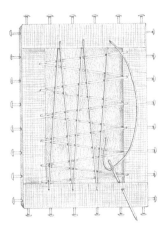

Lace from side to side then top to bottom.

Using a strong needle and a long length of thread, doubled and knotted, lace from side to side across the back of the work, starting in the middle of one side and pulling the fabric firmly with each stitch. Work the long sides first and then the short, keeping the embroidery centred on the card. Continue until the embroidery is completely stretched and securely held. Secure the fabric edges to the card with strips of masking tape.

Oval or round frames

When mounting an embroidery in an oval or round frame, do not remove the centre-marking basting stitches. Using a soft pencil, mark the mounting card (usually supplied with the frame) horizontally and vertically through the centre point. Lay the embroidery face down on a clean surface and match up the marks on the card with the basting stitches. When the mount is accurately placed, lightly pencil around it on the fabric. Now remove the basting threads and cut out the embroidery along the pencilled line. Back the embroidery with lightweight iron-on fusible interfacing and then fuse to the cardboard mount. The embroidery is then ready to frame.

Cut the fabric 2in (5cm) from the pencil line. Lace the edges across the back.

An alternative method

Using the oval or round cardboard mount as a template, trace the shape on to the wrong side of the embroidery. Trim the excess fabric away, leaving a 2in (5cm) turning allowance from the pencil line. Run a gathering thread ½in (12mm) inside the pencilled line. Put the cardboard mount in position and draw up the fabric evenly, adjusting the gathers. Finish with a double back stitch to secure the gathers. To finish, either lace across the back of the work with strong thread or secure the fabric edges to the card mount with masking tape.

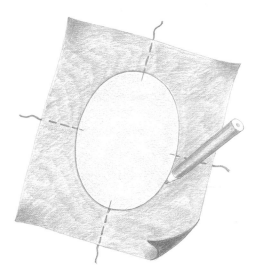

Line up the basting threads and pencil around.

Cross stitch is also a popular canvaswork stitch and is used for making needlework rugs, cushion covers, curtain tie-backs and other furnishings. Worked with tapestry wool on canvas with 12, 14 or 18 threads to 1in (2.5cm), the work can be fine and detailed. On coarser canvas, 10, 8 and 6 threads to 1in (2.5cm), doubled tapestry wool or rug wool is used. Most cross stitch motifs can be interpreted from evenweave fabric to canvas.

GREETINGS CARDS

Small cross stitch motifs are ideal for personalized greetings cards. A small design can usually be worked in just a few hours and, with a little thought, provides a distinctive message that will be treasured by the recipient. Ready-made greetings card blanks with cut-out windows can be purchased in a wide range of sizes and styles. Cards can also be made at home, using thin card or construction paper. Draw the shape of the envelope about ⅛in (3mm) smaller round. Draw shapes to the right and left. Draw and cut a window in the middle shape. Score and fold along the division lines.

Mounting the embroidery

When the embroidery is finished, press it lightly on the wrong side with a warm iron. Trim the fabric so that the motif is displayed centrally in the window.

Spread clear, all-purpose glue thinly around the edges of the window, on the inside of the card. Press the embroidery on to the glue, checking to see that its position is correct before finally pressing down. Fold and stick the left-hand panel over the embroidery. Leave to dry.

Glossary of embroidery terms

Aida a type of evenweave fabric.
Aida band a narrow band of evenweave fabric.
Binca a coarser weave evenweave fabric.
Coton à broder a fine cotton embroidery thread with a high twist.
Count the number of holes per inch (2.5cm) on an evenweave fabric.
Evenweave fabric a fabric woven with warp and weft threads of the same thickness and with the same number of threads in 1in (2.5cm).
Oversewing (overcasting) a stitch used to bind or hem an edge.
Perlé cotton (pearl cotton) a twisted embroidery thread with a high sheen.
Stranded cotton (embroidery floss) a loosely twisted, six-stranded embroidery cotton, which can be separated into individual threads for fine work.
Basting (tacking) large, temporary running stitches.
Wadding (batting) a padding fabric made from either cotton or synthetic material.

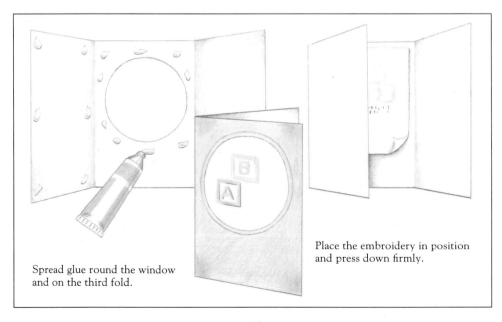

Spread glue round the window and on the third fold.

Place the embroidery in position and press down firmly.

EMBROIDERY STITCHES

Buttonhole or blanket stitch

Working from left to right, bring the needle through from the back of the work on the line where the loop is to be formed. Insert the needle a stitch length away and then back into the line. Do not pull the needle completely through the fabric. Place the thread around the needle tip and pull the needle through, to produce the loop.

Buttonhole stitch

Fly stitch

Bring the needle through from the back of the work and insert again a stitch length away. Pull the thread through leaving a loop between the two points. Bring needle through mid-way between the points but a little lower. Loop the first stitch over the needle, pull down gently and secure with a tiny straight stitch, forming a 'V' shape.

Fly stitch

Long and short
(or encroaching satin) stitch

Work the outline first, using even long and short satin stitches. On curves and at the edge of the shape it may be necessary to alter the stitch length. When the outline is completed, work alternate rows of long and short stitches to build up the design.

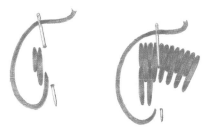

Long and short stitch

Double cross stitch

This is worked as a single cross stitch, which is then covered with a vertical and a horizontal stitch. Sometimes a small straight central binding stitch is made to hold the threads in position. A double cross stitch worked with a central tiny cross is sometimes called star stitch.

Double cross stitch

Long-legged cross stitch

The long arm of the stitch should be twice the length of the short arm. The first longer diagonal of the cross is made upwards from left to right, before completing the second arm of the cross. Unlike cross stitch it is impossible to work the first half of this stitch along the row first. Each cross should be completed before the next is started.

Long-legged cross stitch

MAKING CHARTS

Once you have learned how to work from a chart of coloured squares or symbols, you are ready to begin making your own charts. Do not be discouraged if you want a special design for a picture or sampler. Once your friends and family know that you do cross stitch they will be asking you for all kinds of designs – racing cars, aeroplanes, golfers, tennis players, footballers, swimmers – as well as certain flowers and shrubs and, sometimes, pictures of their houses. None of this should deter you. Making cross stitch charts is simplicity itself.

You need a picture or a design to work from. Pin this to a board and place a sheet of tracing graph paper on top. Usually, this has a scale of 10 squares to 1in (2.5cm). Draw round the main outlines of the picture. Now, using coloured pencils, colour in the squares of the paper, following the design lines underneath. Sometimes, a line will go through a square. This does not matter as long as you keep to the general design outline.

When you have finished, you will have produced a simplified version of the design, the shape converted into squares of colour. Draw a series of coloured-in squares down the side of your graph pattern, one square for each colour.

Now comes the creative part; go through your stock of stranded embroidery cottons and allocate a colour to each coloured square. Snip a small piece off and tape it alongside the square so that you can quickly identify the thread you are going to use.

The next stage is a little more difficult. You have to decide what size you want your motif to be. Each coloured square is going to be a cross stitch. Supposing your motif is 56 squares deep and 84 squares wide. On fabric with a count of 14 threads to 1in (2.5cm), your motif is going to be about 4×5in (10×12.5cm). Using a coarser fabric, with a count of 10 threads to 1in (2.5cm), the motif enlarges to just over $5\frac{1}{2}$in (13cm) deep by nearly $8\frac{1}{2}$in (21cm) wide. Thus, you can work your motif to any size you like, just by choosing the right count of fabric.

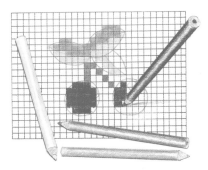

Trace the motif on to graph paper.

Colour in the squares, following the lines.

Symbol charts

Some cross stitch charts are given with symbols instead of coloured squares. You can make this type of chart, using clear sheets of acetate printed with squares. These are obtainable from some draughtsmen's suppliers and art materials shops.

Place the grid over the picture or drawing. Copy each square of the grid on to squared paper, using a symbol for each colour. Here are some symbols you might use, to represent colours.

| ◪ Black | ◩ Green | ◩ Yellow |
| ▬ Blue | ▮ Red | ⊠ Pink |

ASSISI EMBROIDERY

In this variation of cross stitch, a simple motif is left unworked while the surrounding fabric is covered with cross stitches. It is said to have been evolved in the 14th century by the nuns of the convent of St Francis of Assisi in central Italy. You may like to try this variation for yourself, working on a coloured Binca fabric using pearl cotton. A simple motif is given and, by working this in different colour combinations, a set of pretty Christmas tree decorations could be made.

Cut Binca fabric into 3in (7.5cm) squares, two for each decoration.

Work the design on one square in white or black thread on coloured fabric or in coloured thread on white fabric. Each square represents one cross stitch.

Trim with lace and sew a ribbon bow to a corner for a hanger.

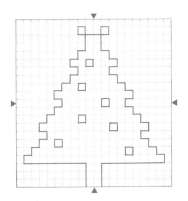

Join up the marks to make a squared chart. Each square is one cross stitch.

When the motif is completed, you can outline it with back stitches in a contrasting colour or metallic thread.

Make up the ornaments by sewing the embroidered square to an unworked square, right sides facing, leaving a gap in the seam. Turn right side out and stuff with toy filling.

Close the seam. Sew gold or silver lace round the ornament. Add glittering beads if you like. Sew a bow of narrow ribbon to one corner for a hanger.

Assisi needlecase

Work yourself a needlecase with an initial in Assisi work. Cut Binca or Aida fabric to a rectangle and work from one of the letter charts given in this book, positioning the initial on the right hand end of the rectangle. Add a decorative border.

Back the embroidery with soft fabric and sew together, right sides facing, leaving a gap for turning. Turn right side out, press and close the seam with slip stitches. Cut two pieces of felt for the needlecase pages, fold and sew inside. Make a loop and button fastening on the edges of the needlecase.

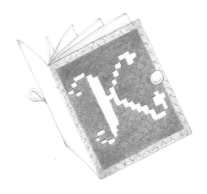

Work an initial on the cover.

NEEDLE POINT

Needlepoint is another type of counted thread embroidery and most cross stitch designs can be interpreted on to canvas, using cross stitch or half cross stitch. Working on canvas is a way of enlarging a design.

If you are planning to enlarge one of the pictures in this book, for a cushion or a rug, it is good idea to copy the design on to squared paper first, deciding how many squares you will cover with each cross stitch. Not all designs enlarge successfully and, by working in this way, you might save yourself hours of wasted work and unpicking later.

Similarly, many of the smaller pictures can be interpreted on to very fine mesh canvas. For this type of embroidery, choose stranded crewel wool, separating and using single strands in the needle. Small, petit point motifs look exquisite on box tops, book covers, needle cases, pincushions and bookmarks.

BLOCKING CANVAS EMBROIDERY

Embroidery on fabric rarely distorts in working, especially if it has been worked in a frame. Usually all that is needed is a light pressing on the wrong side to return the work to shape. Canvas embroidery, on the other hand, often distorts and requires special treatment to return it to shape.

Pull and pin the dampened canvas into shape.

Trim the excess canvas from the embroidery leaving about 2in (5cm) all round. Pin a large sheet of white blotting paper to a board and draw out the finished size and shape of the worked canvas after trimming.

Take special care to get the sides straight and the corners square.

Dampen the finished embroidery on the wrong side (a laundry water spray is a good way to do this). Place the dampened embroidery face up on the blotting paper and gently pull on each of the sides in turn until the embroidery is square and fits the drawn shape exactly. If the canvas is badly distorted, you may have to pull quite firmly on opposite corners to remove the diagonal bias.

Using rustproof drawing pins, insert pins into the canvas in the middle of opposite sides. Working towards the corners, continue pinning until the canvas is stretched and taut and square on the board.

Leave the work to dry overnight.

Half cross stitch This stitch is exactly what it says – half a cross stitch and is the most used stitch in embroidery on canvas. You can use it instead of cross stitch to interpret cross stitch charts.

Work from right to left or left to right, but it is important that all the stitches slope in the same direction. Reverse the direction of working on the subsequent row.

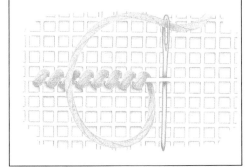

SEWING STITCHES

Sometimes you will need hand sewing stitches to make up pieces of embroidery. Here are the main stitches you will need.

When making up embroidered items, use all-purpose thread in a matching colour so that stitches do not show. A single strand of embroidery cotton can also be used, for oversewing or hemming.

Running stitch

This stitch is used to join pieces of fabric together. It is also used for gathering fabric. Begin with a small back stitch, pick up several small, even stitches on the needle and pull the needle through. If you are working a seam, work a back stitch occasionally to strengthen the seam.

Basting

This is used to hold two pieces of fabric together temporarily. Work it in the same way as running stitch but make the stitches ¼in (6mm) long with a ¼in (6mm) space between each stitch.

Oversewing

This simple stitch is useful for joining the edges of fabric together and can also be used to neaten seam edges to prevent them from fraying. Working from left to right, bring the needle through at A and insert the needle from the back of the work at B, bringing it through to the front at C, ready to start the next stitch. Keep stitches small and evenly spaced.

Gathering

Running stitch is used for gathering fabric. Work as running stitch and leave a length of thread at the end of the row for pulling up the gathers.

Hemming

Hemming is worked from right to left, taking up 2 threads of the fabric at the fold of the hem. Insert the needle obliquely on the edge of the fold.

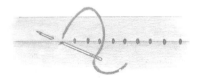

Slip stitch

Work from right to left and bring the needle up through the folded edge of the fabric. Pick up a thread or two on the opposite fabric then slip the needle through the folded edge for about ⅛in (3mm). Bring the needle through and pull gently.

Acknowledgements

The authors and publishers would like to thank the following for their help in producing this book: **Pamela Harper**, Creative Director, H. G. Twilley Ltd, Roman Mill, Stamford, Lincolnshire, for the supply of Lystra threads and fabrics. **Julia Dixon** for working Blue vase on page 24; **Charlotte Dixon** for working Home, sweet home on page 86; **Judi Lang** for working An abundance of fruits on page 50; **Jenny Thorpe** for working Tabby cat on page 46. Also Impress Cards, Slough Farm, Westhall, Halesworth, Suffolk, IP 19 8RN, for supplying blank cards for Loving thoughts on page 64 and the Christmas cards on page 80.

Stranded cotton substitution chart. (There are no substitutes for 176, 177, 183)					
Lystra	Anchor	Lystra	Anchor	Lystra	Anchor
1	1	40	253	76	48
2	352	41	264	77	73
3	366	42	256	78	342
4	376	43	257	79	108
5	378	44	246	80	110
6	355	45	265	81	111
8	304	46	254	82	112
11	36	47	206	83	119
13	309	48	245	84	128
14	901	49	217	85	130
15	890	50	246	86	123
16	820	51	842	87	850
17	891	52	260	88	921
18	380	53	817	91	154
19	359	54	226	92	155
20	370	55	208	93	153
21	369	56	862	95	161
23	276	57	256	97	397
24	358	59	228	98	399
25	365	60	46	99	400
26	347	61	335	100	100
27	308	62	35	102	289
29	891	63	47	103	255
31	305	64	9046	104	212
32	290	65	29	107	340
33	304	66	76	106	382
34	302	67	895	108	19
35	298	68	25	109	44
36	297	69	271	113	188
37	295	70	26	118	189
38	292	73	50	119	2
39	286	75	51	120	275
				121	170